Kristin—
Hope that this year
is a standout one for you
in V-O.
Break a lip!

V-Oh!

—∿—

Tips, Tricks, Tool and Techniques To Start and Sustain Your

Voiceover Career

Marc Cashman

ISBN: 0990395804
ISBN 13: 9780990395805

TABLE OF CONTENTS

DEDICATION

This book is dedicated to my wife, Lola, who's always been my best critic and biggest supporter, and my daughter, Remy, who's been a great production assistant and proudest fan.

PREFACE

Words on a page aren't just words.
They're pictures. Stories. Ideas, emotions, moods and attitudes.

The way you put those words together, how compellingly you tell that story, how you "sing" those words—are what makes a great voice actor.

The thing that distinguishes voice acting from all the other arts is the fact that *you can't see the performer*—you can only hear them. It's like performing in a play—but the audience is blind. They can't see your facial expressions, they can't see your body language or how you move and gesture. The story's almost *solely dependent on your voice*. Yes, they can hear some movements you make—if they generate noise—but overall, it's your voice that commands center stage.

Using that voice with skill evokes a quote by the author Paula Fox that always sticks in my head: "A word spoken as meant contains a mysterious energy that can awaken thought and feeling in both speaker and listener."

That's what I've been doing for over 35 years: working with words spoken as meant. And I'm lucky enough to continue to be on "both sides of the glass"—writing for, casting, and directing top

V-O talent—as well as being directed as a talent in innumerable projects. So I think I've got a healthy perspective on voice acting. As an instructor, I've collected a bunch of tools, tips, tricks and techniques to help any voice talent—from aspiring voice actors to veterans—perform to the best of their abilities.

Over and over, I've seen my students apply many of these tools, tips, tricks and techniques to their voiceover career, and they tell me it helped them book more work and become a better voice actor. If this works for you, I hope you'll write to me to let me know. It would be music to my ears.

FOREWORD

Through my many years of training voice actors, I've found several things that my students have in common when entering the world of voiceover: they were either told (or have convinced themselves) "...you've got a great voice... you should be on the radio (or in cartoons, or doing commercials, etc.);" they have "fallen in love" with the sound of another voice actor's voice or delivery style and want to emulate that "sound," right down to the mic and equipment the actor uses; or they've decided they want to do something fun and creative with their life—and voiceover is either something they've always wanted to do or sounded like something they might want to try.

Regardless of what it is that attracts you to voiceover, the single most important thing you need to know is this: Voiceover is not about your voice, it's not about the equipment you use and it's not something you can just "try" to do. OK... that's really three things, but you get the idea. The bottom line is that if you are going to succeed in voiceover (to whatever degree you personally define "success"), you must have a passion for this type of work and for constantly studying and learning how to be better than you are.

Voiceover is as much a craft and art form as painting with oils. It is not something that can be learned over night, or even in a few weeks. A good voice actor requires performing skills that demonstrate a deep understanding of storytelling, nuance, subtlety, effective communication, and even a little psychology, not to mention a variety of business and technical skills. These are all things that take time to learn. Voiceover is not something for the faint-of-heart to venture into. This type of work can easily be described as the most challenging form of performing. After all, unlike all other forms of performance, the only thing a voice actor has as their tool for telling a story, is the sound of their voice. Nothing more. For that reason, alone, working as a voice actor can be challenging, frustrating, time consuming, expensive, and just plain fun - all at the same time.

But, even understanding everything that goes with it, more people than ever are learning how to work in voiceover—and are becoming successful voice actors. The mere fact that you've purchased this book tells me that you have that passion—or at least a spark of the necessary passion to be a voice actor.

"So what do I do with that passion?" I hear you ask. Good question! If you are starting from scratch, the first thing you need to do is start learning about the craft and business of voiceover. Read books, start taking voiceover, acting and improvisation workshops; attend voiceover conventions and conferences and focus on learning everything you can about this crazy business. If you've already been studying for awhile, congratulations, you're on the right track. Keep at it. Oh, and by the way, you'll never stop learning about voiceover. This is a constantly evolving performing craft.

An interesting thing about learning something new is that the same idea or concept can be taught by several different people, and you might think you "get it," but not really. But at some point, you'll hear the same idea or concept presented in, perhaps, a slightly different way and...WHAM! It's like a light bulb suddenly turning on in your head...It's an epiphany! NOW, you not only "get it," but you understand it!

And that's what this book is all about.

The ideas and concepts Marc reveals in this book are, for the most part, age-old and time-proven. In fact many of the same ideas and techniques you'll read here are covered in other books on voiceover, including my book, "The Art of Voice Acting."

But THIS book might be the one that turns that light bulb on for you.

Marc has done a brilliant job of compiling the techniques and ideas for working in voiceover that has taken him literally decades to gather. Some are "standard" techniques, while a few are "new" approaches to an old idea. But, everything here is valid and works in the everyday world of a voice actor. And, even if you only have a handful of light bulb moments while reading this book, Marc will have accomplished his goal.

Now, your job is to put your passion to work by studying this goldmine of information and applying it to what you learn, have learned, or will learn from other books, workshops, conventions, and private coaching.

Do that...and you can't help but be successful.

—James Alburger, Author (<u>The Art of Voice Acting</u>), Teacher, Producer (VOICE)

INTRODUCTION

This book is a compilation of virtually everything I know and have learned in over 35 years of directing voice talent and being directed in the V-O booth, in voiceover and voice acting.

I make a distinction between the two.

To me, voiceover is the non-acting side of the V-O business: announce tags, legal tags, e-Learning modules, non-fiction audiobooks, public announcements, IVR (interactive voice recordings—"Press 1 to leave a message, 2 to speak to a customer representative...", etc). Voice *acting* involves, well, acting. As in a lot of commercials, animated series, videogames and interactive games, fiction audiobooks. But they both have one very important skill in common: the ability to tell a story.

Telling a story behind a microphone is a lot harder than telling it in person. That's because the audience can't see your facial expressions or body language. *Everything you feel comes out of your mouth.* So, a voice actor has to compensate a bit to bring their stories to life. But they have to do it subtly, with nuance, emotion and all the other myriad skills necessary for a compelling vocal performance.

V-Oh! isn't a how-to book, but it has some how-to elements. It doesn't have stories, but it's got a few opinions. It's also got some defaults, general rules, guidelines and metrics. And it looks at V-O from different perspectives. It hopefully provides some interesting takes (pun intended) on many things V-O; new angles on mastering necessary skills; some approaches on dealing with the business end of things, and some realistic ways of navigating through the Brave New World of V-O in the 21st century.

When I look at the amazing amount of material my colleagues have written about V-O in the past 20 years, I'm honored to be able to add my knowledge to theirs. I hope that the information in this book gives you some new insights, perspectives and food for thought. You'll see how passionate I am about voiceover. I hope this book inspires you to feel the same.

—Marc Cashman, August 2014

FINDING THE MUSIC
IN COPY

You are musical, whether or not you sing or play an instrument. If you listen carefully, you sing when you speak. Don't believe me? Try this little exercise by saying out loud, "I'm feeling great today!" Now, say it with your mouth closed. Do you hear the melody, the notes? The natural inflection you use to emphasize words or phrases is the music of your voice.

Music is all around us. We hum tunes to ourselves all the time. At one time or another most of us have pounded drums, tickled the ivories, sung in a choir, strummed, plucked, blown or wailed. We sing in the shower, we sing in the car. We've sung on Saturday or Sunday morning services, and have followed the notation in the hymnal or prayer book. It's a rare person with a "tin ear." Even someone who can't carry a tune or dance can understand rhythm, and most of us have enough sense of intonation to tell whether a note is sharp or flat, or whether it extends or stops abruptly.

Copy and text are musical. They have different keys; whole notes, half notes, quarter notes, eighth notes. Copy has sharps, flats, rests; words that are held, chopped off, high or low, soft or loud, all the same emphasis or wild ups and downs, with dynamics and crescendos, read slowly and smoothly. Copy reads (or plays) like a story/song, with a beginning, middle and end. Directors sometimes use musical terms to direct voice actors. *Take a beat* means waiting a moment. *Pitch it up* would ask you to raise your pitch a bit. A *staccato* direction would mean hitting words crisply and quickly, sometimes biting into them. *Legato* would suggest you read a phrase or sentence or section slower and smoother.

But there's one thing that copy or text doesn't have—a steady beat or rhythm. Music has a time signature—copy doesn't. Copy has a cadence. Copy—particularly conversational copy—has an ebb and flow. We don't talk in a steady beat. In our conversations, we sometimes talk fast, then slow down; we stammer and stutter. We inflect wildly and project, or make our voices tiny, almost to a whisper.

Sometimes our speech is bit jerky, but that's how we talk. Our job as voice actors is to take written words and turn them into the cadence of everyday conversation.

It all comes down to understanding that words and phrases have specific sounds. Emotive words are the easiest to hear. Say the word "happy." What's the sound of happy? It's bright. It's joyful. It's a word that you automatically lift, like your mouth. Conversely, what's the sound of sad? It's mournful, and it's a word that turns down, as your mouth does. Then there are the sounds of conceptual words, like "hope" or "rejection." The first sounds comforting, uplifting. The second sounds sad and hurtful. There's also the sound of verbs and adverbs: "fast" sounds fast and should be read a little bit quicker, and "slow," well, you get the picture. Adjectives are a gold mine of music, with words like "beautiful," "ugly," "brutish," "selfish" and on and on. Are you starting to hear the music in words?

When you take a musical approach to copy, you'll have a better understanding of the music hidden in scripts. Listen to the sound of your voice in playbacks and hear the variation of "notes" and intensity. Although I advise voice actors to not put headphones on when they're acting (so they're focused more on the performance and don't fall in love with the sound of their voice), I find that actors learn to have more control of their delivery with headphones on. The microphone is extremely sensitive to every breath, every plosive, every note.

Unless you're performing animation or copy that requires a ton of energy and inflection, most professional voice actors stay within a middle range of notes, with occasional highs and lows, and maintain a consistent volume. The more breath control you have (from the diaphragm, and with proper posture), the more you'll be able to hit certain "notes" as you deliver your copy. A number of voice actors have confided that, at one point or another in their career, they had a difficult time delivering a specific phrase during a session, and the director gave them a *line read* (that's how a director wants a word or phrase or sentence to be delivered). If that ever happens to you, don't take it as an insult. Consider it part of the job—it's just an instance where you weren't able to hear the music in the copy—the "notes."

Elaine Clarke, a veteran voice actor and the top V-O instructor in San Francisco, has a great take on this:

"There is music in speech. It lilts up and down to separate thoughts, emphasize key elements, or give directives. Even a monotone speaker lifts and lowers the pitch slightly to separate phrases and add punctuation. It's all a matter of degree. When words are read, many readers forget to apply this natural melody to speech...the problem with reading words on the page is that the words don't naturally belong to us. Often, the spoken words sound read rather than real...What the actor has failed to achieve is matching the way the words would sound had they come out of the speaker's mouth first, before they were typed. As

voice actors, we have to learn to break that acquired habit of sounding like we are reading and learn to speak in a real and natural manner." *

If you want to strengthen your interpretation and give more depth to your performances, whether you're acting in commercials, animation, narration, audiobooks or even e-Learning courses, listen to the music in copy. Listen to voice actors you admire and hear how they sing when they speak. Sing more yourself, each day, to expand your vocal range, flexibility and versatility. You'll soon hear the copy and text you narrate infused with the beautiful music of your voice.

---

* Elaine A. Clark, *There's Money Where Your Mouth Is;* Backstage Books (2000).

TRANSITIONS AND
VOCAL PIVOTS

M ost stories have three parts: a beginning, middle and an end. The space between the end of one part and the beginning of another I call a transition. In that transition, many times you need to perform a "vocal pivot." That's where the tone of your voice changes from one part to the next.

Many commercials are structured like this, in the form of Problem, Solution, and Call To Action. The first part will present a problem: "Do you have problems with _____?" The second part will offer a solution: "Well, now there's _____!" And the third part will tell you where to get the product: "Call 800-GETITNOW or go to getitnow.com today."

In the Problem section, your tone of voice will sound concerned, possibly frustrated, maybe even angry, because you're relating to people who have a problem with a similar product or service. In the Solution section, your tone of voice brightens, sounds positive and upbeat, with a promise of solving the listener's problem. And in the Call to Action section, your tone will have a slightly urgent quality, urging the listener to purchase the product immediately, if not sooner.

See if you can find the transitions in this spot:

If you've struggled to lose weight on your own, you're not alone. Millions of people just like you struggle with it everyday: moms, husbands...hard-working folks. But after years of searching, these people finally found a way to get healthy by uniting their desire to lose weight with a power they knew they could depend on...faith. Introducing Body Shaper...by inspirational fitness legend Bobby Lee Jones. Bobby Lee's secret is incorporating his breakthrough workouts and healthy nutrition with the power of faith. And now, he's made Body Shaper available to you as the first faith-based, in-home DVD workout program. Call 888-BODYSHAPER today. 888-BODYSHAPER. Or got to bodyshaper.com.

You can easily break this spot up into three sections:

Problem: "If you have struggled to lose weight on your own, you're not alone. Millions of people just like you struggle with it everyday: moms, husbands...hard-working folks. But after years of searching, these people finally found a way to get healthy by uniting their desire to lose weight, with a power they knew they could depend on...faith."

This is the first transition. Your tone changes—you do a vocal pivot—from kinda bad to glad:

Solution: "Introducing Body Shaper...by inspirational fitness legend, Bobby Lee Jones. Bobby's secret is incorporating his breakthrough workouts and healthy nutrition, with the power of faith."

Here's your second transition. Now you need to do a vocal pivot from glad to somewhat urgent:

Call to Action: "And now, he's made Body Shaper available to you as the first faith-based in-home DVD workout program. Call 888-BODYSHAPER today. 888-BODYSHAPER. Or go to bodyshaper.com."

These shifts in tone happen frequently throughout all types of copy, from commercials to learning modules to audiobooks. Keep an eye out for them and apply vocal pivoting whenever you have the opportunity.

LISTENING

The art and skill of voice acting is an intricate combination of interpretation and voice control. All the skill sets that comprise great voice acting—articulation, projection, intonation, dynamics, timing, acting, and myriad other talents—are absolutely necessary to be successful in this field. But one skill that you must develop—in classes, coaching, auditions and sessions—is the art of listening.

Many times you can learn more by listening than you can by actually doing. Listening is a critical skill to hone, because it cannot only help you to be objective about your performance, it can help you achieve the nuance, deftness and control that great voice actors possess.

I've found five areas of active listening. You need to:

1) Listen to yourself, but don't listen to yourself. What? Sounds like a contradiction! Actually, this takes a bit of getting used to. When I say, "Don't listen to yourself," I mean don't fall in love with the sound of your voice (my friend and colleague Robin Armstrong calls it "voiceturbation"). Unless you're doing a phone-patch session, or need to hear another actor who's isolated, don't listen to yourself with headphones. When I talk about listening to yourself, I'm referring to your acting, your conversationality (if directed to do so), and your believability. You've got to develop the ability to listen to yourself objectively, and ask yourself, "Do I believe this person?" And, "Is he or she making sense of what they're talking about?" It's a bit schizophrenic, but you need to step outside yourself to determine whether you're connecting with the copy you're performing in a class, submitting as an audition or delivering in an actual session. I ask all of my students to listen intently to their in-class performances (all of which are recorded) to get an objective sense of their delivery.

2) Listen to fellow students. Whenever you're in a voice-acting class or workout group, if you hear anything you like, make note of it and incorporate all the good things into your performance. If you hear a mistake, or something you think is wrong, or don't like the way a particular word or phrase was interpreted, make sure you avoid those things when it's your turn behind the microphone (I call this the "pothole effect"—avoiding a pothole when you see a car in front of you hit one). And most importantly, listen intently to the instructor as he or she directs the other students, particularly if you're going to be performing the same script. Make very specific notes so that when it's your turn at bat, you'll be able to hit the ball out of the park.

3) Listen to the director. Whether it's a class, an audition or an actual session, it's crucial that you listen to the director after each take and incorporate that direction into the subsequent take. If a director asks you to emphasize a specific word or phrase and you don't follow their explicit direction, the director might think that they didn't make themselves clear, and hopefully give you the benefit of the doubt and repeat their direction. But *if you don't incorporate their direction on the following take*, the director will then realize that it wasn't them, it was you, and that YOU WEREN'T LISTENING!

4) Listen to the engineer. What?! Is an engineer as important as a director? Sometimes an engineer can be crucial to your performance, so anything they instruct you to do in the booth, whether it's adjusting (or changing) your microphone and/or your headphones, shouting on or off-mic, working with a monitor, whatever—listen carefully to what they're saying. Like the director, they're there to help you give your best performance possible, and they usually know what they're talking about.

5) Listen to your competition. Who are they? They're on the roster of every talent agency, on the air or in an audiobook. They're narrating websites or e-Learning modules. They're starring in videogames or computer apps. And there's a reason: They've got all the skill-sets a director wants in a voice actor, and they're people you should listen to intently—and emulate. Now, is *everybody* you hear great? No, but there sure are a lot. Yeah, you'll hear a performance from time to time that'll make you say to yourself, "Whoa, how did *that* person get the job? They were terrible!" But that's usually about 1%-2% of the time, and they don't count. If you're just starting out in voiceover, listen to other voice actors on or off-air; listen to their delivery, their energy, their articulation, their acting—and mimic them. Literally, repeat what they're saying and how they're saying it. Listen to their cadence, their conversationality, their believability. And when you're watching TV and a commercial or documentary or cartoon comes on, close your eyes, turn up the volume and *listen*.

6) Listen to narrators you love...and be inspired by them. Listen to their delivery as templates for what your delivery should, and could, be.

SOME QUICK PRONUNCIATION TIPS

I want to clear up a few common pronunciation mistakes:

the

1) The default pronunciation of the word the is pronounced "thuh." You'll say "thee" when the next word following starts with a vowel: "the only thing..." or "the everlasting spirit..." or "the intelligent choice", etc.

a

2) Despite the pronunciation proclivities of the present President and past ones, and seemingly all politicians (self-important speech makers), the default pronunciation of the word a is pronounced "uh" and not the long form of the vowel, "ay." Say "ay" when you're referring to the first letter of the alphabet.

your or you're

Want to make sure you always say your or you're instead of yer? Put an e at the end: yore. Do the same for for. If you don't want to say fer, put an e at the end: fore.

our

Want to make sure you always say our instead of are? Put an h in front of our and you'll always be able to distinguish them.

Other mispronunciations

A few other common mispronunciations (and these have nothing to do with regional accents) I hear from professional voice actors are "axe" for ask, "excetera" for etc., (from the Latin et cetera) and "expresso" for espresso. I still hear "nucular" for nuclear and also hear a lot of lazy double-lls: "probly" or "prolly," "regurly" and "particurly" instead of probably, regularly and particularly. Another very common mispronunciation is with The Arctic and Antarctica. I hear "Artic" and "Antartica"—even from scientists! And sadly, the more I listen to documentary narration, the more I hear the "c" being dropped, so it's possible that the latter pronunciation will soon be deemed acceptable.

The letter W is also somewhat problematic. "Double-yoo"—two u's—is technically how to pronounce the letter, not "Dubya." I once called a local Radio station in Los Angeles, KFWB, and asked them why half of their on-air personalities said, "Kay-Eff-Double-yoo-Bee" and the others "Kay-Eff-Dubya-Bee." They said that the station didn't have a particular pronunciation policy in place. I've got a feeling W will join Antarctica and The Arctic in its relaxed pronunciation.

Here are a few more: it's chipotle, not "chipolte," larynx, not "larnyx," forward, not "foward," memento, not "momento," veterinarian, not "vetinarian," realtor, not "realitor," asterisk, not "asterik" or "asterix" and orangutan, not "orangutang."

That said, I actually encourage the occasional mispronunciation when you're doing a spot that requires a very conversational, first-person, real person read. Saying words like "probly" and "vetinarian"—relaxing your speech a bit—helps you sound more believable sometimes.

ARE ACTING CLASSES HELPFUL FOR VOICE ACTORS?

Yes!

There's considerable call for character voices in videogames, animation and some commercials, and being able to pull off a character convincingly behind the mic can be very lucrative. Also, most voice work requires your natural, "signature" voice behind the microphone. So taking acting classes is a smart choice, especially if you've never had any acting training.

Depending on the instructor, classical acting and improvisation classes can be particularly helpful. They teach you spontaneity, how to be freer and in touch with your emotions. This is very helpful for a voice actor, considering all the emotion is coming through your voice. It prepares you for producers who'll tell you exactly what kind of emotion (and how much) they want exhibited in a script. Acting classes will come in very handy when you're auditioning (and hopefully booking) animation projects, videogames, interactive CD-ROMS, ADR/looping and audiobooks.

Good acting teachers can instruct you in other areas you need for voice acting: cold-reading techniques, vocalization techniques, memorization tricks, dialogue techniques, setting the scene, understanding the back-story, and more. The thing to remember is that we're not so much in the business of voice-*over* as we're in the business of voice *acting*.

Keep in mind that there's a different dynamic between stage and the V-O booth. Some acting classes teach the actor to project their voice so they can be heard in the back of the theater, without the need of a microphone. But when you're behind the mic, it's as if you're talking into someone's ear. Also, being in front of a live audience assumes that they can see your facial expressions, body language and choreography. But in a V-O booth, no one can see you! You have to compensate for that fact by using your voice much more expressively.

GLOTTAL ATTACKS!

Do you unconsciously attack words that start with a vowel? How about your "t/y" or "d/y" words? Here's how to deal with them.

Have you ever listened back to some of your recordings and hear a harsh glottal attack at the beginning of a word starting with a vowel? It's most common on a word that begins a sentence, but not always so. Here are some articulation exercises that highlight this phenomenon:

1) Outside overseers organized overtly, only to outrage overzealous opinions.

2) Inside information is actually inside if individuals are interested in any of it.

3) Everyone attending the art exhibit entered the exit and exited the entrance.

4) Only army ants attack anyone out in the open, unarmed.

How do you eliminate the attack of the glottals? Breathe into them. This softens your entry. We use parachutes to land softly on the ground. Use air to ease into a vowel, and keep the air moving. Breath control is key. When you're speaking, your mouth is open and your words are riding on crests of air, just like you ride on crests of waves when you're surfing.

But instead of riding the wave crests toward the beach, imagine that you're riding the crests parallel to the shore, jumping from crest to crest. That's what you have to do with your breathing. You need to keep generating that air, keeping it going so your voice can "surf" through a phrase or a sentence.

Also, as for the aforementioned "t/y" and "d/y" words, those are word pairings you come across all the time. Examples of "t/y's": that you, what you, must you, put you, etc. When you're not careful, they end up sounding like you're sneezing, like you're saying "choo": "thatchoo," "whatchoo," mustchoo," "putchoo." "D/ys" work the same way, but this time with the sound of "joo": did you, would you and could you tend to sound like "didjoo," "wouldjoo" and "couldjoo." Now, I'm not saying to avoid this sound altogether, because it's very conversational. Just don't get into the habit of always pronouncing words like this, particularly for some corporate, instructional or documentary narration.

THE SOUNDS
OF PUNCTUATION

Every punctuation mark has a sound (or multiple sounds), but not every punctuation mark has a sound reason for being there. Honor punctuation...when it makes sense. If a punctuation mark makes no sense, chances are it's a typo. And if not a typo, then an inadvertent notation. Many copywriters are very specific about their punctuation, and those marks can guide a voice actor. But others are lazy spellers and sometimes get the grammar mangled, and some don't understand how to accurately punctuate copy, no less understand how it sounds. Make punctuation marks work for you. Move them around, add them or ignore them, if necessary. Just make sure that they make sense given the context. And be aware of their sounds, of which there are myriad shadings, depending again on context.

Periods.

A period finishes or closes a thought and finalizes a statement. "That's the way you do it, period." It's the sound of finality—most of the time.

Commas,

Commas continue a thought, so we need to hear the sound of you continuing to say something, as if reading a list: "He picked this, that, and the other thing." Some actors treat commas with upspeak: "He picked this? that? and the other thing." Occasionally it's okay to apply upspeak to one comma, but in the aforementioned example, be judicious.

Question Marks?

Always honor a question mark. It didn't get there by accident (well, occasionally it does), but there are a number of ways to ask a question. Is it a legitimate question that you want to know the answer to? Or is it a rhetorical question, where the sound of the question actually sounds like a statement? Discern which way sounds most appropriate by hearing it in context. Notice I said, "hearing it," not "reading it." Sometimes reading it doesn't make sense. Only when you ask the question aloud do you get the context of how the question should be phrased.

Exclamation Points!

Exclamation points, like question marks, didn't get there by accident. It's the copywriter's cue that they want excitement. Always honor exclamation points and neglect them at your peril. They're there for a reason. When they're in an energetic context, like "Wow!" or "Hey!" or "That's great!" you need to gauge the level of excitement and deliver it appropriately. If you go overboard on the excitement you can end up sounding a bit psychotic. In general, try various levels of enthusiasm vs. excitement to sound more realistic. I like to think of "sincere enthusiasm" as opposed to excitement, particularly in a retail spot. However, you can ramp up the excitement when you're talking to toddlers.

They love hearing the excitement in your voice—that's what gets them excited! (I think of the example of asking your dog if they want to go for a walk. They jump up and down when they see your eyes widen and hear your voice squeal!) On the other hand, when you see exclamation points in the context of negative excitement (horror or terror or danger), you also need to gauge how appropriate your delivery should be.

One of the easiest ways to interpret exclamation points is just to make the word or phrase sound *special*. Just give it a *bit* of oomph—but not OOMPH!

Note: if you know you have to shout a line, take a step back from the microphone. You can also alert the engineer that you have a shout line or a yell line and ask them what the best delivery is for that particular microphone. Or you can ask the director whether they want the shout off-mic, with your head turned slightly. They'll appreciate you asking in advance.

Ellipses...

Ellipses' three little dots are one of the most misused and misunderstood of punctuation marks. First, they denote a pause or a beat. "He really didn't understand...what exactly she was saying." (Q: When a director asks you to "take a beat," do you know how long a beat is? A: It's about as long as it takes for you to say the word "beat.") When an ellipsis is at the end of a sentence, *the sentence is incomplete—it hangs*: "If only I could..." or "She told me never, ever to..." It's also heard in incomplete questions: "Why do you always...?" or "Can you tell me how to...?" The sound of an ellipsis is similar to the sound of a comma, but I call it a comma on steroids. It tells the listener that you're going to continue speaking until you've finished your thought—usually with the next phrase. Ellipses are very common in movie trailers: "Something happened...in this house...in this room...to this girl...that would become the most documented haunting in American history." The problem is, sometimes, that copywriters also use ellipses to signify taking a beat, and they place them all throughout the copy and don't make a distinction between the hanging phrases and the beats. You have to make sense of the two and sometimes replace ellipses with periods to finish thoughts and make the structure work.

Dashes–and Semi-Colons

Dashes, like semi colons, are mini-stop signs. And you can't ignore them. When you see a dash, cut yourself off—literally stop breathing. When you see a semi-colon, apply your vocal "brakes" for a fraction of a second.

(Parentheses)

The sound of parentheses is the sound of an aside, like you're talking out the side of your mouth: "He comes across as a really nice guy (but he's really a jerk)." The sound is sotto voce, Italian for "under the voice" or "under the breath" or "very softly." Words in parentheses should be spoken with just a touch less volume as the other words in the sentence. Another trick for making parenthetical phrases or asides work effectively is to slightly lower your pitch to offset the phrase.

Colons:

Colons are introductory punctuation marks. They set up, introduce or announce the following phrase. Your voice should have the anticipatory sound of an introduction.

"Quotation Marks"

Quotation marks surround a word or phrase with a milli-beat. I call these little marks the "bra" of punctuation: they lift and separate (some words from others). So take a milli-beat before and after the phrase in quotes, or...just use your fingers and do "air quotes" and you'll have the timing down perfectly.

bold, *italics*, <u>underlined</u>, or CAPITALIZED

Although these don't exactly qualify as punctuation marks, the following typographical treatments are in virtually every form of copy and text. Ignore them at your peril! They are words that are in **bold**, *italics*, <u>underlined</u>, or CAPITALIZED forms. They're more cues from the copywriter where they want you to emphasize these words, stress them, lift them, punch them. If you don't, they'll assume that either you're not paying attention or that you don't think they should be stressed, even though the writer thinks otherwise—and purposely made that point in the text. Sometimes copywriters want you to compare and contrast the same word, and they'll use these treatments to get that point across. Like this:

In Kingman, Arizona, folks know <u>this</u> is your guy for transmissions. (*Main Street, transmission guy*)
This is your guy for clogged drains. (*Plumber*)

This is the only way for the writer to convey that they want you to contrast the auto mechanic from the plumber (you could also contrast transmissions and clogged drains a bit). So you'd emphasize the two "this's" but you'd give each one a different intonation. The easiest way to contrast these words is to pitch the second one up slightly.

BUILDING YOUR
VOICEOVER "HOUSE"

N ow, I'm not referring to a home studio. I'm referring to you. In order to build a sound structure (pun intended), imagine a house—your voiceover "house."

What goes down first? You need a foundation. The foundation of all connected voice acting (should there really be any other type?) is sincerity. There's a cynical Hollywood saying that goes, "Always be sincere, even if you don't mean it." But in voiceover, you have to mean it. People can hear sincerity in your voice—or a lack of it—a mile away. It's what gives you believability and makes people want to listen to you.

Next: plumbing, a sewer line, and some rough electrical. So you've got to lay down your metaphorical "pipes" with vocal warm-ups. Then do some basic electrical setup by practicing some tongue twisters to strengthen the electrical synapses in your brain.

Then comes the framework of your voiceover house. The framework comprises all the skill-sets you bring to the micro-phone: breath control, timing, eye-brain-mouth coordination, articulation, consistency, analysis and interpretation, acting and listening and taking direction. It's what gives your house its design and overall structure. And all of these beams have to be equally strong and straight to give the structure integrity.

Next comes the flooring. What kind do you want? Hardwood? Carpeting? Tile? The sound of your flooring is determined by smile. You've got 360 degrees of smile to play with, and depending on what you're describing depends on the amount, or degree, of smile. A total lack of smile—zero degrees, would, I imagine, be pure evil. The opposite—a full 360 degrees, would be, possibly, beatific. You'll never be able to achieve those extremes vocally, so most of your smile falls within the typical bell curve. You just have to determine how much or little is appropriate.

Think of applying it in genres: kid's copy will have a lot of smile, retail commercials a bit less, some corporate a bit less, e-Learning a bit less. But smile permeates everything. I like to think of smile like the background radiation scientists discovered when they explored the origin of the universe and the theory of the Big Bang. Smile permeates the voiceover universe in varying degrees.

Next, what gives your voice house more solidity? The walls. What do you want? Brick? Wood? Stucco? Concrete? Vocally, this is heard in your level of confidence. It's the attitude and energy you bring to the mic. If you're unsure of what you're doing, people will hear it. If you're unprepared, you'll stumble. If you're lazy or unfocused, it'll show. Confidence is the sound of strength and reassurance. And you're confident when you're prepared and know what you're doing.

And what do you do with this framework and all these walls? You connect them. You bolt them to the floor and to each other. And that's what you need to do with the words you're speaking. Notice I said speaking, because that's what you're supposed to sound like—like you're speaking, not reading. And so to sound like you're speaking, and speaking from knowledge, speaking from experience, speaking from the heart, you need to do the same thing you did with the walls. You need to connect. You need to connect with the words and phrases you're describing, and you connect by emoting, by telling a story conversationally, by understanding the sounds of words and phrases that convey feelings, attitudes, descriptions and actions. When you connect with copy or text in this way, your structure is sound.

And what do we want on the walls? Paint? Wallpaper? Paneling? You're going to treat these walls with color, with texture, with shading and depth. That's what you need to do to words and phrases with your voice. Depending on the words (and depending on who we're talking to) our word-colors can be vibrant and glowing, or they can be pastel-like, or they can be more like watercolors, or they can be like oils or other materials—textured.

Finally, what goes over everything to keep it protected from the elements? The roof. And what covers everything you say? Authority. You always have to sound like you know what you're talking about—even if you don't. This is what gives you credibility. But the tone is never an "I know this stuff and you don't" attitude. Your authoritativeness has to be leavened with a welcoming, inviting, reassuring tone, so it comes out as a "sit next to me and I'll walk you through this so it makes sense" tone. This is the way for listeners to trust you, and it's also a reason for a client to keep coming back to you.

COLORING OUR WORDS

I t's hard to remember exactly when we got our first coloring book, but we do remember it was fun. At first, we sprayed crayon colors all over the page, without a care as to whether we stayed inside the lines or not. As we became toddlers, we experimented with finger painting, then crayons and markers, and our coloring started to get more refined. We learned boundaries, we assigned certain colors to certain objects, and were more discerning in our choice of colors. A few years later found us drawing with colored pencils, and we discovered shading and outlining. Later still, we marveled at the results of paint-by-numbers, and then moved on to watercolors and pastels. Some of us continued to pursue art (and still do) with acrylics, oils, watercolors, and myriad other materials.

Those coloring books of our youth were random, assorted pictures, themed pictures or page-by-page pictures that laid out a story. And each one of these pages had the same format: a black outline on a white page that showed a picture. At a glance, we could see a cabin with a chimney near a lake, with a boat tied to a pier with fishing poles at the end, a dusty, winding road leading up toward the cabin, with a big apple tree on the front lawn and mountains towering behind.

As children, we looked at this black and white tableau and made some decisions: the sky would be blue, the cabin would be brown and the lawn would be green; we'd apply the same colors to the apple tree, but add some red for the apples; the road might be brown or charcoal; the lake would be blue, the mountains might be gray, brown or dark blue and the sun would be yellow. We colored in the outline of a story.

As adolescents, we got better at drawing and making color assignments. Our sky might be bluish-purplish. We'd add clouds that might have shades of gray and green; the water on the lake would be a mixture of many colors, reflecting the sun in its ripples and the boat that floated on it; the road might be a mixture of black, brown, dusty tan or beige, with black rocks and pebbles strewn about; the cabin would have a different colored roof, and, like the apple tree, cast shadows from the light of the sun.

As we grew older and more sophisticated with colored pencils, watercolors and markers, we'd start adding depth and shading, because we could discern perspective and light better. And we'd spend much more time at our task; we were more exacting and meticulous.

And so, from a simple outline, we colored a weathered cabin on a sparkling lake, smoke rising from its chimney; a beat-up boat tethered to an aging pier, with a dusty and somewhat rocky dirt road leading past the cabin, a big, shady apple tree on its front lawn, majestic mountains towering behind the cabin, framed by an intensely blue sky dotted with puffy clouds and a welcoming sun.

This is what we have to do when we're telling a story.

Printed words are groupings of black symbols on white paper. Strung together intelligently and creatively, they tell a story, just like the outline of a picture in a coloring book. It's our job as voice actors to color the words that need coloring, to give them depth, shading and perspective. We do that by using all of our tools: voiceprint, vocal techniques and acting abilities.

The reason that most great stage and screen actors are believable is because we can see their characters. We can see their body language, their nonverbal movements and gesticulations, and their eyes. We see them embody characters through their words and actions. We can even see them think! But people can't see voice actors—they can only hear us. We have to compensate by bringing color and emotion to the written word, and that comes through just one place—our voice.

The nuances of the human voice are extraordinary. Millions of years of human evolution have made the sound of the human voice a wonder to behold and something no machine will ever duplicate. They've tried, though. At first, people thought that developing speech recognition would be a simple matter of replicating phonemes, and they've been successful in transplanting those basic sounds into many applications. But like astronomers exploring the universe, the more speech recognition developers peer into the vastness of speech "space," the more they realize how complex it is, because the human voice is so incredibly unique. Our vocal cords hold a powerful gift: the power to paint pictures, with an infinite variety of colored shades, textures, depth, patterns and mixtures. We have the innate ability, through our voice, to convey meaning without even uttering a word! And of course, the power to elicit so many emotions.

Some voice actors refer to themselves as voice artists. Well, then: if we're artists, we have to take out our palette of vocal colors and brush those words and phrases with the most appropriate colors; we need to wash them, brush them, tint them and dab them. We have to channel vocal impressionism, cubism, pointillism, abstract art, op art and realism into our phrasing. We have to apply the endless color combinations of emotions and infuse them into words.

We're blessed with the ability to lift words off the page effortlessly and to articulate them clearly. But if we don't inject emotional depth and real meaning into them, if we don't artistically color in the outlines of those pictures, we'll never do justice to beautifully crafted text or copy, or capture a listener's attention. We'll waste a great opportunity.

So, when you're presented with copy or text that cries out for coloring, take out your 120-count box of vocal crayons with all their wonderful hues and shades and create a masterpiece!

CREATING A BACK STORY

One of the most important—and easiest—things you can do to sound conversational is to start the conversation beforehand—establishing a back story.

I do this almost every time I get behind the mic to perform a commercial spot, particularly when I have to read copy that's awkwardly written or full of advertising-ese: ad copy that's chock full of ad buzzwords and phrases that we'd never say when talking to each other on a day-to-day basis. Let me give you an example with this spot for a grocery store:

Age range 25-55, upbeat, conversational, happy, sincere. Spot is about saving money on groceries, but should not be condescending. Matter of fact. [:20]

There's always one sure way for you to tell if you've gotten a great deal. When you can buy more for less! Now, that is true savings!

At Balboa's, that's something we want you to experience every time you shop. And, we're so proud of the savings we can offer you...

That we draw attention to it on every receipt!

Balboa's...It means a Great Deal!

Look at all the ad phrases and copy points: "a great deal' (mentioned twice), "when you can buy more for less," "true savings," etc. They're not particularly conversational, yet that's what the spot calls for. So how do we put a conversational tone on this kind of copy? Set up a back story by asking three simple questions:

1) Who am I? You can tell who you are by reading the copy: "...that's something we want you to experience every time you shop. And, we're so proud of the savings we can offer you...That we draw attention to it on every receipt!" The word "we" tells you that you work for the company. If you ever see "we" in copy, as well as "our" or "us," you know you're the spokesman for the company.

So where are you in the company? In the corporate offices or in one of their stores? Chances are you're in the store. And if you're in the store, what's your job title? Cashier? Stock boy? Produce clerk? No! These people are too busy with their departments. There's only one person who's got the big picture of what the store offers, and that's...the manager! Which leads us to the next question:

2) Who are you talking to? Well, if you're in the store, who else would you be talking to? A customer, of course! Possibly a new customer, maybe a local customer who takes advantage of Balboa's savings. Which leads us to...

3) Where are you? Another no-brainer: in the store!

Okay, so now that you've established who you are, who you're talking to and where you are, you got a good sense of place and purpose to establish a simple, credible back-story. This is a story that you'll say out loud. You're in essence going to create a make-believe mini-conversation before the copy starts—take a beat—and then launch into the copy.

Now the story's got to make sense. You can't be setting up the copy with a non sequitur, like, "Gee, it's raining outside." (beat)

"There's always one sure way..." It's got to be a realistic setup. Something simple, but something that leads up to the first line. So if you're the manager talking to a customer in the store, you might invent a mini-story like...

Mrs. Jones:	Hi, Mr. Cashman, how're ya doin' today?
Me:	Great, Mrs. Jones, how 'bout you?
Mrs. Jones:	Super. Say, remember when we met you told me how much money I'd save shopping at Balboa's?
Me:	Sure do.
Mrs. Jones:	Well, I just wanted to show you my receipts from the past three months. I saved over $300!
Me:	Wow, that's terrific! As a matter of fact, I *do* remember telling you that...(beat) There's always one sure way for you to tell if you've gotten a great deal. When you can buy more for less! Now, that's true savings!

By coming up with a mini back-story, you've established the conversational tone that'll carry over into the stilted copy you've got to impart. In fact, whenever we have to make awkward copy sound good, I call it "Silk Purse Productions." The whole point here is warming up before you jump into copy cold.

There's a simple analogy here. Have you ever stayed in a cabin on a lake during the summer? If you have, the lake usually had a pier jutting out from one of its shores, and sometimes there'd be a little floating island not far from the edge of the pier that you could swim to.

Now imagine it's very early in the morning, and you're standing at the very edge of the pier, with your toes curled around the edge, your knees slightly bent, ready to jump in the water. The water's smooth as glass—and very cold! But you jump in anyway, and when you come up...you're freezing! The water's cold, cold, cold! Why? Because you didn't warm up before you jumped in!

Now, let's rewind this scene. This time, you're in the cabin, it's early in the morning, but you tiptoe past your cabin-mates, slowly open the front door, slowly close it, and look at the lake with anticipation. Then...you run across the porch, run down the stairs, run down the lawn, run across the beach, run down to the end of the pier...and then jump into the water! You come up and...Ahhh! The water feels great! Why? Because you warmed up before you jumped in!

You can do this with lots of copy. If the copy calls for a ton of energy, rev up before you dive in. If it calls for you to be quieter and thoughtful, sit on a stool and start the beginning of a nice, quiet conversation. Whatever the direction calls for, *establish the tone before you start reading* and you won't be halfway through the copy before you're warmed up.

BEING BELIEVABLE

One of the hardest skills in voiceover is developing the art of being (or sounding) believable—throwing the announcer out of your voice and sounding like a normal, everyday person. A lot of these skills can be stolen directly out of an on-stage or on-camera actor's notebook, because they're not dependent on the printed page. When you have copy in front of you, it's comforting to fall back on—you don't have to memorize the words like actors do. But most of the time, those actors sound believable because they've internalized the lines they're saying—without having the "crutch" of the words in front of them. Here are a few tricks you can use to get to sounding "real."

- Rehearse, rehearse, rehearse. The more you internalize your part, the easier the copy will flow and become part of you.
- Punctuate with pauses, changes in pace and of inflection, dynamics, emotional attitude, vocalized sounds, non-verbal utterances and other subtleties.
- Allow scripted punctuation marks to guide you, but don't take them literally if they don't feel right.
- Allow the lines of a script to flow into one another as they would if you were telling a story to another person, not reading it. In other words, make your performance as conversational as possible.
- "Lift" your lines instead of reading them, i.e., look at the line, then say it, looking at the director or engineer if they're with you in the studio.

- Add your personal spin to make the copy your own.
- Don't become so focused on your character that you lose sight of the whole story.
- Don't exaggerate your character's attitude, speech patterns, or other characteristics, unless the script specifically calls for an over-the-top characterization.
- Speak your lines to one person or a few, real or imagined, expecting that they'll respond. Pretend you're speaking to your best friend or close relative.
- Underplay, rather than overplay. Louder isn't better. When in doubt, pull back, speak softer and be more natural. Sometimes less is more.
- Keep your body posture in a stance consistent with the character you're playing.
- Don't read! Talk *to* the audience, not *at* them. Enunciate, but be careful not to over enunciate.
- Break up the cadence of the copy.
- Speak as quickly as you would if you were talking to someone and speak as you would in a real conversation, what I call "conversational speed."
- Ad lib where appropriate.
- Give yourself a realistic lead-in to the front of the copy.
- Stay in the moment. Pick up cues. React to other performers (if there are any), and don't allow any air between your line and theirs, except when it makes sense to pause.
- Understand the message in the commercial, your character's role in it, and your relationship to other characters.
- If you're going for a "real person" character, keep your delivery flatter and thrown away.
- Keep your brain-eye-mouth coordination working on all cylinders.
- If the copy has short sentences, memorize each line and deliver them without looking at the page.

TREATING CONJUNCTIONS

Conjunctions abound in ad copy and text: And, for, to, with, but, from, so, if, etc. Sometimes they start sentences, many times making them incomplete, (causing English teachers much consternation), or sometimes they end them. Here are a few guidelines for dealing with conjunctions:

1) If a conjunction starts a sentence, don't emphasize it unless it's treated (in bold, italics, underlined or capitalized). Spring into the word or phrase after it. In the sentence, "And Bob decided to do something about it," take the stress off "And" and place it on "Bob."

2) Many times conjunctions are part of lists. With a line like "Now you can get shirts, pants and jackets for 50% off!" The "and" between "pants and jackets" doesn't need to be emphasized. The "and" is read almost like "an'" "'n" or an actual ampersand (&). Consider a conjunction placed this way as a bridge between words, where the words or phrases on either side of the conjunction are stressed.

3) What's the exception? When the writer italicizes, underlines, bolds or capitalizes the conjunction. In the sentence, "You'll get $1,000 off AND free inspections for a year," the "and"

is emphasized because the writer treated the word that way specifically. When you see that application in scripts, make sure to follow the writer's cue. It's their way of giving you a bit of direction without actually being there.

DEALING WITH PRONOUNS

Pronouns are another tricky thing to address in copy, because many times it's not clear if or when they need to be emphasized. Most of the time you can determine their emphases if you understand the context of a given sentence. Let's look at a few examples. In this copy for The Oil Depot, there are a number of pronouns:

V-O: The people who tell you to change your oil every 3000 miles...change oil for a living. The people who tell you to change your oil every 5000 miles? They sell cars for a living.

"You" and "your" in these lines are understood—they don't need to be emphasized. If you did, you'd be implying that it's okay to change *your* oil, but not someone else's. The phrase that needs emphasis here is "change your oil." Let's look at the next couple of lines:

V-O: But the people you can trust to give you the right oil change schedule based on how, what and where <u>you</u> drive? They work <u>here</u> for a living. At Oil Depot.

The first two "you"s don't need to be emphasized, but the underlined "you" does. That's pretty obvious—the writer made that unmistakable in the copy. But this next line doesn't have anything italicized, and one "you" still needs emphasis:

V-O: Where our trained experts and exclusive Oil Analyzer will give you the one number...that's right for you.

In this sentence, "our" and the first "you" don't need to be emphasized, but the last "you" does, because of the context. *All* spots are all about you—what the advertiser can do for you, how the product or service will help you—but you don't always have to emphasize "you."

A simple trick you can use to determine the correct emphasis is to read the copy to yourself first—not out loud—before you mark your copy. Let your brain do the work of determining where the emphases lay. Then mark your copy accordingly, if you have any question as to what pronouns to stress. Just remember, most pronouns are a given. Of course we're talking to you, him, her, they or them. We just don't have to emphasize those pronouns all the time. Here's one more example:

V-O: We take the time to know you. Your goals. Your dreams. So we can tailor what we do...around what you do.

The first "you" and the next two "your's aren't emphasized. *Know, goals* and *dreams* are the appropriate words to stress here— the active words—and the pronouns are a given. In the sentence, "So we can tailor what we do...around what you do," the first "we" doesn't need to be stressed, but the second one does...as well as the following "you": "So we can tailor what *we* do...around what *you* do."

As usual, emphasis is determined by context, where sometimes pronouns are stressed—but most times not.

ENHANCING COPY

There are little words and phrases that are the glue that holds a lot of our conversations together. And these same words and phrases can be used to help soften some copy that's rigid or relax copy that's formal. Here's a good example:

V-O: The people who tell you to change your oil every 3000 miles...change oil for a living.

The people who tell you to change your oil every 5000 miles?

They sell cars for a living.

And the people you can trust to give you the right oil change schedule based on how, what and where *you* drive?

They work *here* for a living. At Oil Depot.

Where our trained experts and exclusive Oil Analyzer will give you the one number...that's right for you.

Drop by the Depot. Oil Depot.

Once you've determined that it's appropriate to enhance copy, you need to do it judiciously. So, for this copy, you could insert "Y'know" in front of the first line, "And" in front of the second line and "Well" in front of the third line. But there's something in the next line that doesn't make sense: "And the people you can trust to give you the oil change schedule based on how, what and where *you* drive?" *And* the people you can trust? That doesn't sound right. They're telling you that you can't trust the oil change people and you can't trust the car dealers. So "And the people you can trust" needs to be changed to..."*But* the people you can trust." Now you've got a sentence that makes sense: you can't trust the oil guys, you can't trust the car guys, but you *can* trust us. So the copy, enhanced, reads like this:

V-O: Y'know, the people who tell you to change your oil every 3000 miles...change oil for a living.
And the people who tell you to change your oil every 5000 miles?
Well, they sell cars for a living.
But the people you can trust to give you the right oil change schedule based on how, what, and where *you* drive?
The work *here* for a living. At Oil Depot.
We're our trained experts and exclusive Oil Analyzer will give you the one number...that's right for you. Drop by the Depot. Oil Depot.

Most V-O actors are loath to change even an iota of copy because they're afraid of ruffling the copywriter's feathers. They think it's the height of hubris to be manipulating copy that's been approved and is ready for air. But a decent copywriter is going to see right away that changing the "and" to a "but" in this spot makes sense. And chances are, 99% of the actors who audition for this won't be discerning enough to notice it. But when you do, the writer will think one thing: this person gets it. He/she had the intelligence to understand the story and the context, and temerity to give the copy a little flourish, and put their unique spin on it.

Oh, sure, there'll be some writers who might be miffed, even angry that you altered one syllable of their precious copy, but trust me, they're few and far between. Most writers want good actors performing on their spots, and the best ones encourage actors to make their copy sing.

FINDING THE SUBTEXT

Initially, when you're first learning how to navigate ad copy, you tend to focus on what I call the *mechanicals,* the physical skills you need to sustain a professional delivery: articulation, breath control, eye-brain-mouth coordination (that's that loop of taking in words through the eyes, rummaging around in the brain and exiting through the mouth) and minimizing mouth noise. Only once you've mastered the mechanicals are you able to start injecting some acting into voice acting.

Here's an analogy: learning to drive a car. When you first learn how to drive, you concentrate foremost on the mechanicals: how to turn the wheel and steer the car and how to use the gas pedals and brakes. Once you've gotten the hang of those physical movements, you then learn how to honk the horn, tune the radio, adjust the mirrors, fiddle with the windows—all while you're driving the car. Then, with those skills and more under your belt, you're able to carry on a conversation.

I call it being on autopilot. So just like driving a car, when your voiceover mechanical skills are so entrenched that you don't have to worry about them, you're able to concentrate on acting. And once you can do that, your job is to tell the story compellingly. You do that by finding the subtext.

The dictionary defines subtext as "the underlying or implicit meaning, as of a literary work," or "a message which is not stated directly, but can be inferred." In ad copy, the subtext is sometimes stated, but most times isn't. However, if you know where advertisers are coming from, you'll almost always be able to find the subtext and deliver the right tone. Let's look at an example where the subtext is actually stated in the copy. It's in this spot for Oil Depot. Can you find it?

V-O: The people who tell you to change your oil every 3000 miles...
change oil for a living.
The people who tell you to change your oil every 5000 miles?
They sell cars for a living.
And the people you can trust to give you the right oil change schedule based on how, what and where *you* drive?
They work *here* for a living. At Oil Depot.
Where our trained experts and exclusive Oil Analyzer will give you the one number...that's right for you. Drop by the Depot. Oil Depot.

What's the subtext? *Trust.* Look at the story. They're telling you that you can't trust the oil-change people, you can't trust the car dealers, but you *can* trust Oil Depot. Understanding that trust is the underlying theme—even though the word is halfway through the copy—lets you inject that tone from the very beginning.

Many advertisers use trust as a basic theme. A big one is financial institutions, because Wall Street is a gamble and financial stuff is confusing and overwhelming. When you're considering investing your hard-earned money, trust in an investment company is the one thing you need to sleep well at night. Another industry that talks about trust is healthcare. Hospitals are scary places. They want you to trust that they know what they're doing when it comes to your health. Others products and services employ trust because they're tied to safety: baby products, cars and tires, insurance, etc.

But there's another common subtext in ad copy: *pride.*

Pride is the emotional foundation of countless commercials as well as non-broadcast messages. It's the pride in a job well done, the pride of being able to help people, to contribute something to society; it's the pride of working for a company that contributes to the better good, makes a quality product, respects its employees, and sets a great example for others in the industry. Corporate spots, many times referred to as "anthems," have pride woven into their banners—they're waving the corporate flag. So even though you might not see the word pride spelled out in copy, like trust was in the spot above, keep an eye (and an ear) out for it.

Trust. Pride. What else? There's a sticky word floating around in marketing circles lately: *delight.* Smart advertisers try to elicit a positive emotional response from customers. They hope that using their product results in a delightful experience. So by infusing a promise of delight in your tone, that alone could entice the listener to act.

Another feeling that's embodied in a lot of spots is the feeling of *comfort.* Literally. What's the sound of someone easing down in a comfortable chair? Aaaahhh. Immediately, you feel relaxed, and that feeling comes across when you talk about a product or service, getting folks comfortable with the idea of using it.

There's one final idea that permeates a ton of ad copy, and it's not a feeling—it's an action. An *invitation.* Virtually every spot you voice is an invitation to try the product or service—even though it may sound like a command. "Drop by the Depot—Oil Depot" is technically a command, but it's also an invitation. Keep this in mind when you're voicing a spot—imagine extending your hand and welcoming someone in. Your smile will be unmistakable—and genuine.

FINDING THE SERIES
OF THREE

A copy or text phenomenon I call the "series of three" is some-thing to keep an eye—and an ear—out for. They abound in ad copy especially. You'll see it in lists, like in retail spots: "Shirts, jackets and pants are all on sale!" Or if the advertiser is describing the benefits of a product, saying it's "quieter, smarter and faster."

Whenever you encounter a series of three, make sure each one of the items (whether they're objects or attributes) sounds slightly different from each other. If you hit the same note on each word, they all sound alike. But they're not. Here's an example:

V-O: At American Bank, we work to help you find the easiest way to reach your goals. In your branch. In your business. In your life.

You can treat "In your branch. In your business. In your life" as a small series of steps, each word going up a note, as if you were walking up the stairs. Or you could split the difference and go up two stairs and going down one. Sometimes a series of three has the same words, like in this spot for a fitness club:

V-O: The idea is to sweat here. And here. And here.

The last thing you want to do here (pun intended) is be repetitive—making each "here" sound the same. Each word needs to have a different intonation or note, to reinforce to the listener that there are different muscle groups.

Lastly, the series of three lives in the literal series of three, like when a commercial counts off the benefits of a product, as in this copy for a moisturizing soap:

V-O: All natural LanoSoap treats your skin to a silky smooth feeling because 1) it's made with Lanolin; 2) it's florally scented, and 3) has natural moisturizers.

You could take a "good, better, best" approach to this series of three, or you could mix it up. Bottom line: make each thing in a series of three sound slightly different.

GETTING THE EMPHASIS RIGHT

A re you able to understand the proper emphases as you read through copy? Do you find yourself mis-emphasizing words? Here's a little trick you can use to make sure you're emphasizing the right words in the right place:

Before you rehearse your copy, read it to yourself—silently. As you go through the script, *let your brain make the emphases.* Underline the words your brain emphasizes, and afterward, read the copy out loud and follow your marks.

You've trained your brain to make the right choices when you're reading to yourself—it understands context. Just like your brain hears the voices of different characters as you're reading fiction, or makes sense of ideas and concepts in non-fiction, unless you have some degree of dyslexia or have something else going on in your brain or vision, it should be able to identify all the words that need emphasis.

One general rule of emphasizing lies in how to emphasize a word that's repeated, whether in the same sentence, another sentence or another paragraph. Usually, the first time you introduce a subject, you emphasize it. But after you've introduced it, most times you'll need to emphasize the subject's descriptor. Usually it's an adjective, but sometimes it can be an adverb, verb or a pronoun. An example:

V-O: Supposedly, he had a great-great-grandfather who had stolen a pig from a one-legged Gypsy, and she put a curse on him and all his descendants. Stanley and his parents didn't believe in curses, of course, but whenever anything went wrong, it felt good to be able to blame someone.

The subject, curse, should be emphasized the first time you introduce it. The second time it doesn't need to be emphasized. The emphasized word should be "believe." Next is an example where a verb—sniffed—needs emphasis. But the second time it's mentioned, "Another" needs to be emphasized.

V-O: The velociraptor sniffed. It jerked its head and looked right at Tim; Tim nearly gasped with fright. Tim's body was rigid, tense. He watched as the reptile's eyes moved, scanning the room. Another sniff.

Speaking of pronouns, the same holds true. Once you introduce a pronoun, there's usually no reason to emphasize it again, unless it's placed in a context that requires emphasis. Look at the following copy:

V-O: At Oil Depot, our trained experts and exclusive Oil Analyzer will give you the one number...that's right for you.

The first "you" doesn't have to be emphasized—it's understood you're talking to you. But the second you needs emphasis—every advertiser wants to help *you*.

GIVING DEPTH TO WORDS

I'm constantly amazed by how many voice actors deliver their words with awesome articulation and precise projection, but detached delivery. They're quite adept at lifting the words off the page effortlessly, but fail to take the opportunity to color words or phrases with the appropriate attitude or emotion. They sometimes forget to use their acting abilities to give depth and dimension to the words they speak.

In voice acting, all our emotions and attitudes come through our voice. People can't see our eyes or our body language like they can on stage or in film. The slightest nuance in the tone of our voice can convey myriad feelings; non-verbal utterances can convey even more. There are so many places in copy where we can really give the words the depth they need by feeling the words we're saying and injecting emotion into them.

An example that came up in one of my classes occurred when we were working on a spot for a regional hospital, and one word that kept occurring was "hope." Ask yourself: what does hope sound like? When you say the word just by itself, out of context, you tend to naturally say it on a down note. Hope. One word, spoken with a period after it. But think about what hope means. Hope means to cherish a desire with anticipation, to wish for something, with some amount of expectation. It could be something you long for that's realistic or unrealistic. It's an attitude or feeling that could be attainable. And in the context of a hospital, and the feelings it evokes in potentially life-threatening situations, it's a word with a very powerful meaning.

So in this context, hope is an uplifting concept. It always has been. So it's literally a word we need to lift, because the attitude is a positive one. When we say this word, we need to have hope in our heart in order to have hope in our voice. In a spot or narration for a hospital, or any medical facility, the word "hope" needs to be infused with compassion and total sincerity.

On the other end of the spectrum, I hear the word "pain" a lot in copy, and I hear it thrown away. But this is another opportunity to inject the appropriate emotional tone. When you're talking about pain, and you're a sympathetic or empathetic person, and you say the word "pain" you should be wincing a bit. A listener should be able to hear it in your voice. Want a great example of how the sound of *one word* can provoke an emotional response? Think about this: How many times have you called someone you know, *and just by the tone of one word they use to answer the phone*—"Hi"—you can tell if everything's okay or something's amiss. It'll provoke you to either say, "Hi, how're ya doin'?" or "Are you alright?" If one word can get that kind of response, just think of how thousands of your other spoken words and phrases are perceived.

There are innumerable words that you can color and give depth to whenever you come across them. These words are loaded with attitudes and emotions. Don't throw away the opportunity to infuse these words with the appropriate color, feeling and attitude. When you say the word "excitement" or "exciting," deliver it with an exclamation point! (An exclamation point is the only punctuation mark I know that literally connotes an emotion—excitement!) When you talk about how a particular company cares, "care" should be delivered with concern and compassion. Whether they're nouns, verbs, adjectives or adverbs, don't throw these words away! For voice actors, words are easy to say and lift off the page effortlessly, but the listener needs to hear some thought and feeling behind those words. When you really start thinking about them, words are easy to bring to life when you say them with the appropriate feeling or attitude. Here are just a few:

Friendly, elegant, patriotic, confident, sultry, scary, stiff, sensual, helpful, funny, concern, evil, tiring, appetizing, sad, cautionary, breathless, wacky, tough, delicious, carefree, perky, nervous, stuffy, mellow, heroic, magical, cute, bored, sly, exciting.

In my classes, I have my students say these (and many other) words with their accompanying meaning (and sound), and also have them say them with their opposite meaning (and sound). It's funny to say "friendly" in an angry tone. It's funny to say "confident" in a wimpy way! And when you do this exercise, it becomes clear that, as voice actors, when we speak, we're painting a picture for the listener, compensating for the fact that they can't see us saying what we're saying.

A lot of the copy you get as a voice actor will not be chock-a-block with words and phrases that you'll be able to get behind emotionally. There's not much emotion in "2.9% APR financing for 60 months on all vehicles in stock." But the next time you *do* get some copy to perform that has any kind of thoughtful theme, sit with those words for a minute. Feel the emotion behind the copy. Find the emotional resonance behind the words you're saying. I guarantee you that you'll start performing turning those two-dimensional words on the page—into three dimensions.

SHORTENING OR EXPANDING
YOUR TIME

M any times (particularly with advertising copy) you'll need
to shorten or expand your read by a few seconds. This is
because the allotted time is specific (:10, :15 or :30 are usual) and
the copy has already been approved to go to broadcast. Here are
a few tricks to shorten copy:

1) Contract wherever possible. Look at this copy for a bank,
which is running a little long for a :30:

Direction: Conversational

V-O: Most people are pretty happy with their bank. You put
your money in, you take money out. And people don't think about
changing where they bank until there is some sort of problem.
Maybe they start charging higher fees or they have changed so
many times you don't even know them anymore. If this sounds
like you, think about BD Financial. We would love to meet you.
The minute you walk into BD it will put a smile on your face. We
are rated one of the best-run financial institutions in the country.
And we have been around for 60 years now. Discover a better way
to bank, at BD Financial.

Since they want it conversational, the first thing to do is contract everywhere—consistently. "...until there is..." becomes "until there's." "...or they have changed..." becomes "they've changed," etc. *You* can contract copy if *they* already have, which they did in the third sentence: "And people don't think about changing where they bank..." They didn't write, "And people do not think about changing where they bank." They contracted "do not." They just forgot to contract the other places that needed it. So, if you're pressed for time—or just want to have a better audition—contract words that need contracting. You'll sound better, regardless.

2) Find places to "marry" sentences. "We are rated one of the best-run financial institutions in the country. And we have been around for 60 years now" doesn't need the period in between: "We're rated one of the best-run financial institutions in the country and we've been around for 60 years now" flows and sounds much better and saves half a second.

3) Take out extraneous commas. It takes about quarter of a second to honor a comma, and lots of commas add up.

4) Sometimes it's just a matter of speeding up your pace.

5) Shorten the space between sentences.

The best way to lengthen copy is to be thoughtful and not be afraid of silence. Don't be afraid of taking an occasional beat. I never met an actor who was loathe to take a dramatic beat. Sometimes, depending on how conversational the copy is, you can occasionally stretch your phrasing out or repeat a word now and then, giving you those extra couple of seconds. Sadly, there's much more of a call to truncate our reads rather than linger on them.

GET THE POINT!

One of the many topics I cover with my voice-acting students is navigating punctuation marks in copy or text (I make a distinction between copy—the words and phrases used in advertising or promotion (called copywriting)—and text, the words spoken in narration.

Punctuation marks can be easy or difficult to navigate for some voice actors, depending on their skill and depending on how good or bad the writer is in using punctuation correctly. And while the period, comma, colon and semi-colon can be used fluidly, the question mark can be used many different ways and narrating quotations marks takes a bit of skill in timing, the one punctuation mark that needs to be honored and should never be ignored is the exclamation point.

I can't count how many times I've heard voice actors ignore exclamation points! And I don't understand how they miss them! They're impossible to ignore! There's no other punctuation mark that makes its presence known as well as the exclamation point! (Okay, I'll stop with the exclamation points for now.) Granted, copywriters use them liberally, particularly with retail or direct response copy: "Do it today!" "Call now!" "But wait, there's more!" But that's no excuse to miss them or pretend they're not there. The writer placed them there on purpose—they didn't plant themselves on the page by accident! Oops—did it again!

Exclamation points are used for just one purpose: to convey excitement! Sorry, I just had to use one there. When you see exclamation points in copy, that's the writer's way of telling you, "Make this sentence exciting!" (Oh gee, I did it again).

An engineer I work with, who has listened to thousands of voice actors, recommends bringing a pocketful of exclamation points the next time you have a piece of retail or direct response copy to perform, and, if they're not embedded in the copy, liberally sprinkling them over the page. Sometimes there are sentences which don't have exclamation points that need them, but too many sentences with exclamation points will start sounding silly after a while.

Just how much excitement should an exclamation point convey? It needs to be appropriate to the product, situation and audience. Exciting copy for young kids for a race car toy is going to be read differently than exciting copy for a casino aimed at adults. There are so many different degrees of excitement—the amount of excitement and projection varies in myriad situations: shouting in a stadium, "All right, a home run!" or ringside at a boxing match, "Knock him out!" Exclaiming "Happy Birthday!" or "Happy New Year!" at a party. Seeing someone take a fall and exclaiming, "Oh my gosh!" or accidentally knocking something over and apologizing, "I'm so sorry!" Calling to your kids, "Dinner's ready!" or hailing your neighbor from your porch, "Hey, haven't seen you in a while!" Then there's hushed excitement, when you lean over to whisper to your friend or relative or spouse at an opera or a recital, "I been waiting for months to see this!" Confessing to a loved one, "Oh, you're gonna love this!" or fighting with them, "You never listen to me!" Sometimes excitement goes into the realm of terrorized or insanity!

Here's a tip if you see a lot of exclamation points throughout a spot: be careful not to get too excited—unless you're talking to little kids. They love excitement, and we love getting them excited, too. But you can't get too excited when you're talking to adults—your peers. Too excited sounds a bit psychotic. I like to think of exclamation points as conveying sincere enthusiasm. The best way to approach exclamation points in that context is just to give the phrase that ends with them some oomph. It'll sound sincerely enthusiastic. Plus, if you're being directed in a session, the director will explain the appropriate energy you need to give exclamation points in the script. Just don't ignore an exclamation point. Honor it and give it its due. Get the point!

AUDITIONING IN YOUR HOME STUDIO

V-O auditioning and its protocols are changing, now that home studios are becoming ubiquitous. If you've put together a home studio, or are planning to soon, you'll most likely be submitting auditions with your recording software via email or uploading them to various sites.

If you still drive to a casting company, independent studio or your agent, you usually have two to three takes max and you're done. In your home studio, you can do as many takes as you want until you feel you've "nailed" it. But there's nobody to direct you—this is a totally self-directed exercise, with no feedback. Doing this myself for a number of years has given me valuable insight into the process of auditioning and submitting from your studio. Here are a few things to keep in mind and a number of things to do to prepare you, both physically and emotionally, for this process:

- *Warm up your voice before you record.* Do whatever vocalization exercises you need to do before you enter the booth—just like you would for a live audition.

- *As with any audition, go over any directions, mark, rehearse and time your copy before you record.* Rehearse your copy speaking at the volume you'll be performing the spot. If the spot requires a lot of energy, read standing up, and don't forget to use your hands and arms to help you with emphasis and projection. But if the spot asks for a relaxed, laid-back read, consider sitting on a stool.

- *If a job asks for an audition, audition the copy provided.* If you don't have time to audition, don't send your commercial demo. You won't be considered. Clients have a very difficult time making the leap from your demo to their copy.

- *If you have a number of different auditions to record, first record the ones that are on the low end of your vocal scale, i.e., the deepest ones.* Your voice is most resonant first thing in the morning, because you haven't been talking for 6-8 hours. Proceed to the scripts in a higher key, then finally to any scripts that require a louder sound, or, say, a textured voice or gritty character.

- *If a job gives you a description or direction, follow it.* Read any directions carefully, and give the client at least one take the way they want it. Then, if you want, record a second take the way *you* think it should be.

- *If you don't match the casting specs, don't embarrass yourself or waste your or the client's time by attempting to cast yourself in a role that's obviously not even close to what they're looking for.* For instance, if they ask for a young, 20-ish voice, don't audition if you're 60+. Be objective enough about your voice to pass on an audition that's not right for you.

- *If a client asks you to label a file in a specific way, follow the instructions <u>to the letter</u>.* Be especially cognizant of details like upper and lower case, spacing, underscoring, hyphens, etc. If there are no labeling instructions, ask your agent if there's any particular way they'd like the file labeled. If not, label your files generically: *YourName-Product.mp3* or the reverse: *Product-YourName.mp3*. Every casting director has his or her own way of managing file names, and if you don't pay close attention to the template they give you, you can rest assured your audition won't be considered. If the template shows a dash, use a dash, not an underscore. If the template shows all caps or upper and lower case lettering, *follow the template!*

The reasoning is simple: If you can't follow simple labeling directions, they won't expect you to be able follow real ones in a session! Lastly, if a client asks you to slate your name at the top, just slate your name! Slate it clearly, and follow any slating instructions carefully—some ask for a slate before the audition, some after.

You don't need to give your life story. Keep the slate short and sweet, and get right to it. Don't give your phone number, don't give the client's name, and don't give a pitch! As long as your name is labeled correctly on the file, that's enough information!

- *If you haven't been given the proper pronunciation of the product or service, ask your agent to provide it—or look it up.* If the client hasn't provided it, try looking it up online to see (or hear) how the name is pronounced, or call them if you can locate them. If you still don't know, take your best guess.

- *Have water in the booth at all times and drink in between takes.* Stay hydrated. It truly helps to cut down on mouth noise. I even recommend a nasal rinse before you get behind the microphone, which helps abate adenoidal deliveries.

- *Record your auditions at 128 kpbs (or 96 kpbs if it's a particularly long audition) Mono.* You don't need a stereo file for an audition, and you want to try to limit the size of the file you're emailing. If the file is really big, arrange to upload it (Hightail. com will allow you to upload 100 MGs free!) instead of trying to attach it to an email. You'll know if the file's too big when it bounces back with a "cannot be delivered" message.

Some voice actors use watermarks embedded in their auditions—a sound effect or music bed used to protect your work. Stephanie Ciccarelli of Voices.com explains:

"While the Internet provides many opportunities for securing work, it has also unfortunately been used as a means of stealing creative products, including voice-over demos. This is particularly true of custom demos of shorter scripts such as telephone voicemail boxes and commercials. People who steal work are only a small margin of Internet users, but over the years, voice talent and other freelance creative professionals have learned the hard way, often by hearing their audition pieces used commercially without being paid for their services."

Voices.com even provides members with watermarks and sound logos. Watermarks can be placed in various places in your audition or used throughout. Many clients, however, find watermarks distracting.

Many voice actors, instead of watermarking their auditions, will alter the script slightly, either omitting some copy or changing vital information like phone numbers or website addresses. If you do use a watermark or opt to not use one but alter the copy slightly, make sure to make note of it in your cover letter that accompanies your audition, so the client understands that you're protecting yourself and that you didn't misread their copy.

- *If the script is a :60, submit one solid take.* If it's a :30, submit two and show your range. If it's a :10 or :15, submit three. If it's an animation audition, read the directions carefully, decide on your character's voice and commit to it.

- *If you're using an audition service, you should know that there are a lot of voice actors out there with great equipment in their home studios, with a great sound.* Check, double-check and triple-check your recording settings before submitting your audition.

Make sure your recording is like Goldilocks: not too soft, not too loud (no distortion), but just right. Send some of your sound files to people you know in the business who can give you feedback (no pun intended) and constructive criticism about the sound you're getting out of your microphone and booth/recording space. Bottom line: if your audition sounds like crap, forget about being considered for any job, because most clients can't make the leap. If that's the case, get your recording system tweaked before you send out any more funky-sounding auditions.

   - *Make sure you're recording in a dead-sounding space, where the sound isn't bouncing off hardwood floors or high ceilings.* You can do a lot to dampen the sound around your microphone. Many times, if you have some basic soundproofing, your auditions will sound great, and can be used as a final track. Remember that you're competing with professionals who've been in the business a long time, so your sound needs to be competitive. You could have the most expensive microphone and gear in the world, but if you're recording in a space that's too alive, you'll sound bad. Conversely, you could have a lower end mic that sounds great if the space is dead.

   - *If a job asks you to submit a specific demo, i.e., Commercial, Narration, Audiobook, whatever, make sure your demos or the demos you've posted on the audition service sites are competitive.* If you want templates, go to my website to hear some of the demos I've produced for my students. If your demo isn't competitive, you'd better think twice about submitting yourself for a job, because a lot of other demos out there are going to make yours sound amateurish, and that's the last thing you want.

   - *Listen to your playback objectively.* Do you believe the person you're hearing? Be honest. If not, record it again...and again, if necessary. If you capture a convincing performance, send it on. If not, pass on it. It means you're just not connecting. Don't worry, though—there'll be plenty of others down the road.

- For auditions going to agents, a cover letter isn't necessary, but you should always attach one to every audition that goes directly to a client. It should not only have all the necessary information, like your name, phone number and email address, but it should clearly state what you're auditioning for, the reasons why you'd be a great candidate for the job, and where they might be able to listen to other examples of your voice work. If they want you to submit a quote for your services, be as explicit as possible given the job description, and address any ancillary costs involved, such as studio costs, phone-patch or ISDN charges, etc.

- There are many factors that determine who is hired for a voice acting job—voiceprint, acting ability, rate quote, turnaround time, studio equipment, availability. But your first impression—how well you sound, how well you follow directions (slating, acting, labeling files, etc.), can help a potential client decide quickly whether they're dealing with a pro or an amateur. Performance is important, but always pay attention to the details of the presentation. Good luck!

LIVE AUDITION & SESSION
DOs & DON'Ts

Once you start auditioning for voice work, you'll find that there are a lot of things to keep in mind, and a number of things to do to prepare yourself, both physically and emotionally, for this process. Here are a few tips to remember for live auditions and/ or sessions:

DO:

Preparing outside the booth:

- Practice facial exercises and vocalizing in the car on the way.

- If it's a live audition, arrive at least 15 minutes early to de-stress, warm up, check your call time, go over any directions, mark, rehearse and time your copy.

- Carefully read all directions that accompany the casting specs and times, scripts, and anything else the director has posted.

- Rehearse your copy standing up or sitting on a stool and speaking at the volume you'll be using in the booth.

- If it's a partner read, find your partner and rehearse. If your partner's not there, try to find someone else who's waiting for their partner and rehearse with them.

Preparing Inside the Booth:

- Bring your marked copy into the booth. If you need to wear headphones, place them initially around your neck. If you put them on your ears and there's accidentally massive feedback, your eardrums could rupture. There's usually a talk-back speaker in the booth, so the engineer can talk to you with or without your headphones when he/she needs to.

- There are times when it's not necessary to wear headphones, and I encourage people to avoid wearing them when they can. I think earphones heighten the form when we should be concentrating on the substance—the performance.

- Rehearse your copy at the level you'll be performing it until the engineer asks for a level. Continue reading your copy until the engineer says "thank you." That means they've gotten the proper level on your voice and you can shut up for a few seconds.

- Listen to any instruction the engineer might have for you regarding the microphone.

- NEVER touch the microphone unless the engineer gives you permission. You can, however, adjust the music stand for your copy and request lighting and temperature adjustments.

- If the music stand isn't high enough for you, fold over the top of your copy and hang it over the top of the stand. If that's not high enough, get a couple of big paper clips and a big magazine and clip your copy onto it, raising it as high as your chin.

- Keep the copy at about chin level and make sure you have a good line of sight and plenty of light on your copy.

- Have water in the booth at all times.

The Session:

- Ask for more or less gain in your headphones, if necessary.

- Ask questions about pronunciation of proper nouns or anything that affects your performance.

- Listen to the producer's directions carefully, and be sure to incorporate them into your next take.

- Be attentive. Listen—to yourself, the director and/or the engineer.

- Try to be objective about your performance. Are you believable?

- Redirect nervous energy into constructive performance. Keep breathing and focus on performing.

- Be confident in your abilities. Remember, you were invited to be there.

- Make the copy your own. Inject your personality and unique storytelling ability.

- Take your copy with you when you're done.

After The Session:

- Thank the casting agent or director and engineer when you leave.

- Leave a current demo if appropriate, with your cell phone and/or pager number.

- Leave quickly and quietly—a professional exit.

- Keep track of your expenses—the IRS requires detailed records.

- After you're home from the audition, get names and email addresses for your mailing list for follow-up thank you letters and holiday cards.

DON'T:

- Dawdle. Be ready to read quickly.

- Gab with other actors until after the audition—concentrate and focus on your job.

- Touch any equipment (the music stand is okay). Let the engineer or producer make mic adjustments.

- Argue about direction. Ever.

- Be afraid to make suggestions if the copy is awkward, but don't be surprised if they're not accepted.

- Worry about making a mistake. That's what pick-ups are for. But don't make too many mistakes, either. Omitting words, reversing words, replacing words or swallowing important words should not be an issue.

- Call after the audition to ask who booked the job. If you didn't get called, you didn't book it.

- Criticize your own performance during the audition. And don't make excuses for a poor performance.

- If you're compelled to do a post mortem, do it in the car after you're done.

- Ask for advice or critique of your work—this isn't the time or the place.

- Ask if you can audition again—this is your only chance.

- Bring an active cell phone or pager into the booth. Let it roll over to voicemail.

- Start acting until a beat after the slate, whether your own or the engineer's.

- Ask for a playback of a particular take or the final, accepted take (s).

- Cough or sneeze into the mic.

- Say "Testing, one, two, three" when asked to give a level. Read your copy at the volume you'll be reading the spot.

- Expect to do more than one or two takes. Any more is a gift.

- Wear noisy clothing or jewelry. Also, don't wear strong after-shave or perfume.

- Yell or scream into the mic. You can approximate volume without yelling. If your copy calls for real shouting, back up a step or turn away slightly. And work with the engineer so that he/she can get a level.

- Be afraid to ad lib, but if directed to read the copy "as is," do so.

SKILL AND ART

Voice actors have to multi-task when they get behind the microphone, combining two basic areas: mechanical skill and interpretive art. These areas are reflected in my Report Card, but they need to be combined in order for you to give an effective—and competitive—performance.

Mechanical Skills

These are the areas that require physical movement of organs and muscles: Breath control, Articulation, and Eye-Brain-Mouth Control. These skills need to be on auto-pilot. If you struggle mastering any of these skills, it will impede your read. The best analogy I can give is what was involved when you first learned how to drive a car. Initially, you had to master the mechanical skills: turning the steering wheel, pressing the gas pedal and pushing on the brake pedal. But after a short while, these skills became second nature, and soon you were on "auto-pilot," which then allowed you to talk to others in the car, turn the radio dial, read road signs, talk on the phone (in states where it's legal!), keep your eyes on the road and avoid colliding with other cars, objects, etc. The same holds true in performing copy. Master the mechanicals, get them into auto-pilot mode, and you'll be able to concentrate on the interpretive part: acting. If you haven't mastered the mechanicals, you'll be stumbling through copy and have no chance to bring your acting into the picture.

Interpretive Art

Once your mechanicals are in place and strong, you can concentrate on acting. These are the areas of Analysis and Interpretation, Acting, and Taking Direction. This means sizing up the story and making sense of it, determining what the most appropriate delivery is, and making a choice as to how you're going to accomplish it. But it also involves listening: listening to the director and listening to yourself. There's an art to listening, and the more carefully you listen, the more successful you'll be in your performance.

Overlapping Areas

These are the areas of Timing and Consistency. There's both an art *and* a skill to pulling these off. Reading to time, pacing, picking up cues, and varying your cadence require a combination of skill and art. The same with consistency: staying on track from take to take, timing-wise, tone-wise and character-wise (if it involves characterization).

Putting It All Together

Remember that at least half the people in voice acting today *are actors.* They've been formally trained in stage and theater, and have had extensive vocal training as well. Many of them have mastered most, if not all of the areas I delineate in my Report Card. However, if you fall into the other half—non-actors—you can still increase your V-O opportunities by taking an acting or improv class, if for anything else, *to improve your storytelling ability.*

The great thing about mastering the skills and art of voice acting is that usually, the more you practice, the more adept you get at it. I can't begin to tell you how many people I've worked with who started out completely at sea in voiceover, and within a few short years were able to stand toe to toe with pros. They say "practice makes perfect," and though you may not be able to get there all the time, occasionally you'll nail a performance that's pitch perfect.

THE "TALKING
TO YOURSELF" VOICE

When you see the word "introspective" in script direction, it usually means employing the "talking to yourself" voice. It's the equivalent of thought balloon in cartoons, or thoughts in italics in a book. Sometimes, depending on production values, this voice is filtered with a reverb effect, to heighten the thought balloon concept.

This voice is just above a whisper because it's not a secret. But if you talk too loud, you'll sound like you're off your meds. It's a voice that's audible but not projected. I can think of three common scenarios that evoke the sound of talking to yourself:

1) Looking in a mirror. It's the voice that says, quietly, "Hey, you're lookin' pretty good"—or conversely (as you squint your eyes, looking at some blemish on your face) "What the hell is *that*?!?"

2) Shopping. Imagine you've been given a list of things to buy at the store. As you walk down the aisle, looking for the items, you're talking, quietly, to yourself: "Okay, let's see, cookies, soft drinks, snacks..." If you talk out loud—too loud—in public, you may hear over the store P.A. system, "Crazy person in aisle 5. Crazy person in aisle 5."

3) Christmas morning. This scene involves you muttering to yourself as you try to navigate directions under the words, "Some assembly required" for a toy you bought for your kid. "Okay, let's see here...connect A to B...B to C and...C to...*what*?!?" Again, talk too loud and family members will think you're losing it.

The volume and projection of the talking to yourself voice is between a whisper and normal conversational tone. Some directors call it a stage whisper. It requires you to constantly push air over your words, softening them, like a cloud. It can also be used in a couple of other situations: when you're reminiscing about something, or having an intimate conversation, as if you were talking to someone you're holding close (while you're dancing) or laying next to you.

THE DREADED
"RADIO VOICE"

As a voice acting instructor and coach, I encounter a number of people, mostly men, occasionally women, who've been in Radio for some time and want to transition into full-time voice acting. And they seem to have one thing in common—the dreaded "Radio Voice," which voiceover talent agents shy away from and occasionally, if they hear their V-O demos, run screaming from their office.

What accounts for this aural phenomenon? Well, a few things. Many radio DJs, announcers or personalities wear headphones while they're on the air (they have to, in order to hear cues from the director as well as themselves), and have basically fallen in love with the purring, resonant sounds of their own voice. That's one of the reasons they got into Radio in the first place—plus, many people commented that they loved their voice. Most have been urged by their program director to deliver station-written and produced copy in the same style that they talk on the air, because that's what the advertiser wants and is paying for. And many Radio talent have listened to their predecessors for years, and have consciously or unconsciously emulated them.

But on-air talent have a ton of skill-sets that many agents in the voiceover world don't appreciate. They have superb eye-brain-mouth coordination, i.e., they're able to lift words off a page effortlessly, without stumbling over any words, rarely omitting or adding any, giving them the appropriate energy. They're also able to speak very fast, with outstanding articulation, and an amazing ability to "shoe-horn" seventy seconds of copy into a sixty-second spot. They understand how to deliver the copy points of any ad, and deliver consistently. On-air personalities are also able to ad-lib extremely well, particularly in testimonials, giving advertisers a lot of bang for their buck. But most incredibly of all, they're able to do all these things *live*, with thousands, hundreds of thousands or possibly millions of people listening to them. That's a tremendous amount of pressure on a person, something that most professional voice actors rarely, if ever, encounter. They've got an audience of maybe a dozen people maximum hanging on their every word.

I explain to my students that the aforementioned skills are vital to a professional voice actor, and, truth be told, many of the Radio talent I work with trying to transition into voice acting are able to find their niche. I also remind my students that not everyone is cut out to be an actor. I know a lot of voiceover people doing a ton of non-acting work: announcing, corporate narration, e-Learning and instructional modules, phone-on-hold systems, pre-recorded announcements, etc., and they're making quite a nice living. I know a lot of announcers who come into the studio for fifteen minutes to record a legal tag for a campaign and make more money than the the individual actors in different spots because the tag is tacked onto all of the radio and TV spots in the ad campaign.

But what can a Radio talent do to not sound like a "typical" Radio talent? A lot of on-air folks have a challenging time transitioning into voice acting because they haven't been trained in V-O or taught how to act. So first, take some voice-acting classes or coaching sessions. Learn how to navigate a lot of different kinds of copy and delivery styles. You could even take acting or improv classes to learn how to give even more depth to your performances. Second, don't audition with your headphones on. In a session, sometimes you have no choice (if you're doing a phone-patch or ISDN session and need to hear the director from another location, or you're in a dialogue or trialogue in separate booths). But listening to yourself in your phones puts your voice-print under a microscope—where you end up hearing all kinds of mouth detritus and you end up compromising your performance. And third, work on delivering copy in the same way you talk to people (or pets) you love—your siblings, your kids, your spouse or girlfriend/boyfriend, your parents—just not the way you talk to your listening audience. Believability comes in sounding like you're talking to just one or a few persons, preferably someone you know who fits the target audience you're talking to. You might find out, through classes or coaching, that you've got a lot of skill-sets that can help you make that transition and hopefully lose the dreaded "Radio Voice."

THE FIRST SENTENCE

T he first sentence of virtually everything you read is crucial, whether it's the first sentence of a spot, or of a chapter. Here's why:

1) It usually sets up the story. And in many commercials, the name of the product or service is mentioned in the first sentence, calling for a bit of "billboarding." So slow it down about 2%. Just on the first sentence. It *lets the listener know what you're talking about.* If you speed through it, they won't. Just be a tad more deliberate. You have to be with voiceover, because the listener can't see the copy like you can. After that, you can pick up your conversational pace.

2) It usually sets the overall tone. If you've determined the subtext of the story (trust, pride, hope, etc.), establishing that tone from the very first sentence is important. It's an attitude you'll need to be consistent with from the get-go.

3) It usually tells the director whether you've gotten off on the right—or wrong—foot. It not only establishes your tone, but also your projection, volume, smile, articulation, energy and strength, anchored from the beginning.

But there are always exceptions to the rule. For instance, if the script calls for you to be talking extremely fast throughout the entire spot, then you obviously wouldn't slow down a bit.

ONE WAY TO SOUND LIKE
YOU'RE NOT READING

One way to not sound like you're reading is to develop solid eye-brain-mouth coordination. Good E-B-M is the ability to lift words off the page effortlessly—in through the eyes, rummaging around in the brain and out through the mouth. How can you strengthen your E-B-M? Practice, practice, practice. Read cold copy aloud, a half-hour every day. Read book passages, newspaper or magazine articles, comic books, the back of cereal boxes—anything that you haven't read before. And record yourself! Listen back and try to be objective about your delivery. Ask yourself: does this person sound "read" or conversational?

There are other indicators that you're reading: if you're stumbling through copy; if you're hesitant or not confident with your flow and cadence; if you're separating words or chopping up phrases, instead of breathing through them; if you're over-articulating; if you're breathing too much (struggling to get the words out). All of these scenarios will make you sound like you're reading.

I encourage you to devise a back story, because you need a reason to say what you're saying, and a person or persons to talk to in a setting that makes sense. If you don't envision a scenario in your mind where it would be natural to say what you're saying, then you're talking in a vacuum, saying words out of context. But if you imagine yourself in a setting where it makes sense to say what you're saying, then you've legitimized yourself and the copy and made yourself (and your role) believable.

Another reason it's important to set up a plausible back story is to establish a conversational *tone*, particularly when the copy is stilted and you're saying words and phrases that you'd never say in a typical conversation. If you're in conversational mode, that'll help you navigate easier through advertising-ese. Here's an example of what I mean. Let's look at this copy again for Balboa's (see "Creating A Back Story" for more notes):

Specs: conversational, not condescending, matter of fact, upbeat.

V-O: There's always one sure way for you to tell if you've gotten a great deal. When you can buy more for less! Now, that is true savings! At Balboa's, that's something we want you to experience every time you shop. And, we're so proud of the savings we can offer you...that we draw attention to it on every receipt! Balboa's...it means a Great Deal!

This spot is loaded with advertising-ese. Phrases like, "When you can buy more for less! Now that is true saving!" is typical advertising copy, where you'd never utter these words in a conversation in this lifetime! But you've still got to make them sound conversational. So ask the three questions: Who am I? Who am I talking to? And where am I? You can tell who you are immediately when you see the word "we." "We" means you work for the company. The best role for this would be a store manager, someone who interacts with customers all day. Next, to whom are you talking? Obviously, a customer. So you'd pick someone in your mind who you know, who fits that target audience (in this case, 25-55 year old women), and pretend they're a customer. And where are you? Well, it just makes sense to be *in the store.*

So you're a manager at a Balboa's talking to a customer in the store. Now you've got a reason to say what you're saying. What's a plausible back story? Well, looking at the copy that talks about showing savings on every receipt, I can make up a simple pre-conversation that goes something like this:

W: Hi, Mr. Cashman, how're you doin' today?
Me: Fine, Mrs. Jones. Thanks for asking.
W: I'd like to show you something if you have a minute.
Me: Okay.
W: When I moved here a few months ago and I came into the store, you told me that I'd save a lot of money shopping at Balboa's.
M: I remember.
W: Well, look at these receipts: I saved over $200 in the past three months!
M: Wow, that's terrific, Mrs. Jones. Y'know, I remind all my customers...that there's always one sure way for you to tell if you've gotten a great deal. When you can buy more for less! Now, that's true savings!

Notice what I did: I took a beat just before the copy started. I established a mini-conversation to ease me into the copy. And I contracted "that is true savings" to "that's true savings." I can do it because the copywriter has done it everywhere else in the copy, starting with the first word! That's another way to sound conversational—contract words that need contracting—particularly when it occurs elsewhere in the copy.

And here's one more trick to sound like you're not reading: don't read! Whenever you come to a tag line, a cut line or a slogan at the end of the spot—for instance, "Balboa's...It means a Great

Deal"—don't read it! Memorize it and then say it. Lift your eyes off the page and speak it with sincerity. There's no reason you need to read a few words. Stage actors do this all the time when they're rehearsing a play and trying to get "off-book"—memorizing their lines. They glance at a short line, retain it, and speak to the person in the dialogue or, if it's a monologue, imagine speaking it to someone in the audience. But they deliver the line without having their eyes on the page. So from this point on, there's no reason to read a short tag line at the end of a spot.

MARKING /
ORCHESTRATING COPY

M arking your copy is crucial to every read you do—make the time to do it. Reading an unmarked script at an audition or session is risky. To many voice actors, marking a script is like reading a map. To actors with a musical background, it's like orchestrating the copy. Read the copy through at least twice to get a sense of the melody and cadence, where you take breaths, pauses, emphases. Place your marks above, below, on the side of, in between, through and around words or phrases.

Follow the copywriter's cue. Wherever the copy is **bold**, CAPITALIZED, <u>underlined</u> or *italicized*, stress it. But feel free to add or delete punctuation marks, and add words or phrases that you think will enhance your character and make the copy flow better. Don't be afraid to re-arrange words if they seem awkward. Insert ad-libs if you feel inspired. Many times the copywriter later incorporates it, and it makes you stand out in casting decisions. Phonetically spell out (in capital letters, if you need to) the client's name, geographic places or foreign words. All non-verbal cues should be in parentheses, i.e., (laugh), (sniff), (sob), etc. Emotions (happy, sad, afraid, etc.) can be circled. I also write "T" and circle it when I find a transition. Make sure to write everything *in pencil*. I advise against writing in pen or highlighting in color. If you're using paper, mark with a pencil or with a stylus on a tablet. Your character assignation may change; your initial interpretation of the copy may differ from the director's, and the copy will probably change during the session; it's impossible to erase ink or colored marking fluid. Practice marking copy on magazine and newspaper articles. Here are some marks I use. Feel free to add or adapt any of them to your set of hieroglyphics.

/ Take a breath. Some actors use a comma. This is important for run-on sentences, or sentences with a lot of technical jargon.

// Pause. For a longer pause, you can use ///, or if you have room, a dash (—).

~~ Modulate your voice. Add vocal interest by wavering the sound: bending, pinching, scooping, sliding or stretching a word/note.

↑↓ Inflect up or down, either on a word or syllable. If it's a phrase or a sentence, extend the tail on the arrow.

[ ] Taken as one complete phrase.

___ Stress/punch.

☐ Billboard. This is usually the product name.

! This means excitement! Add more (!!!) depending on the level of excitement!

...? Use a question mark for a hanging question.

( ) A parenthetical statement/aside (to be dismissed quickly, usually *sotto voce*)

⌐¬ Stair-stepping: stepping up or down to enumerate points.

T   Transition.

---- Stretching out a word.

HOW VOICES ARE
REALLY CAST

E ver wonder what's behind the decision-making process of casting voices? Wouldn't you love to be a fly on the wall, listening to the wrangling that goes on behind the scenes of a voice-casting pow-wow? After casting thousands of voices for commercials, narration, video games and countless other V-O projects, I can tell you, you'd be surprised by the truth.

Most companies listen to dozens, if not hundreds of auditions, searching for just the right voice to represent their product or service. A lot of V-O folks think that only the first ten or twenty auditions submitted are considered, and the rest are thrown away. I've not only cast thousands of commercials I've written and produced, but I've sat in on scores of agency-produced casting sessions where I've seen and heard the process first-hand. And I'm here to tell you that most of them listen to all the submissions, in the pursuit of finding that perfect voice.

I work with V-O pros around the world, and a number of them wonder why they're not working as much as they used to, and also wonder if or what they might be doing wrong as a result. And after listening to their performances, I hear that for the most part they're not doing anything wrong! The reason they weren't cast was because of their voiceprint—the sound of their voice.

Everyone's voiceprint is unique, just like fingerprints. No two voices sound exactly alike. When companies cast for voices, the thing that's foremost in their mind is the sound of the voice. They ask themselves, does this voice represent the product or service? They're listening for that magic match of voice talent, copy and product demographic (target audience). They're listening to the actor's resonance, pitch, volume, inflection, projection and personality—all the characteristics inherent in an actor's voiceprint.

Only once they've whittled the auditions down to the top five or ten or so do they start scrutinizing the performance, the match-up of the actor and the copy delivery. Then they listen intently to the actor's articulation, conversationality, interpretation and sustainability. They're listening for a performance that "wows" them, that makes their copy sing.

The discussions that ensue are sometimes relevant or totally arbitrary. The creative director of an ad agency might prefer one actor, while the president of the company they're representing might favor a different one. And once they come to a decision, the CEO's wife could change all that by preferring someone totally different—like a celebrity!

The bottom line: they either like the sound of your voice and think it's a match, or they don't. And if they think your voice *could be* a match, then they compare you to a few other actors who fit their profile and then determine who the best actor is. So if you think having skills are irrelevant, think again. They're what make the difference between you being chosen or tossed.

There's a saying in the car business: "There's a butt for every seat." The same is true in the casting business. So although your V-O skills may be top notch, they're not always going to get you the gig. Genetics—your voiceprint—are a crucial part of the casting equation.

PICKING A VOICE
ACTING CLASS

Voice-acting classes are proliferating throughout the U.S. and other cities around the world, but there are probably more voice acting classes in Los Angeles, because there are more work opportunities there for voice acting. There are Radio and TV commercials, animated series and documentary narrations; promos, movie trailers, ADR and audiobooks; live announce events, Radio imaging, website V-Os and video games; corporate videos, training films and company messaging systems, among many, many other projects. All these productions make L.A. the center of the voice acting universe.

Class lengths and costs vary widely, as do topics. But of the dozens of classes offered, how do you best choose the one that's right for you? Here are a few guidelines and questions to ask:

<u>How experienced is the instructor?</u> - Is the teacher a former or current voice actor? Casting director? Producer? Does the instructor teach all the classes or have substitutes? Are experts from other areas of voice acting brought in to enhance the information given in class?

<u>Where are the classes held?</u> - Are the classes taking place in a professional recording studio, where voiceover projects are produced on a regular basis, or are they held in a living room or classroom?

What is the basic setup? - Is the recording equipment professional? Is there a dedicated engineer, and is he/she experienced? Are you recording to cassette tape, CD or a hard drive for later download? Is feedback between takes recorded for your subsequent review?

How many people are in the class? - Too many people in a class guarantee that you won't be getting much mic time. Ten students are the max a three-hour class should have.

Are the students in each class on the same level? – It's a little uncomfortable when beginners are lumped in with professionals who already have demos or agents. It's intimidating to beginners and not fair to students with more experience.

Does the instructor take just anyone? – Experienced instructors screen prospective students to make sure that they get the most out the course and that they don't have reading problems.

Do materials accompany instruction? – Are handouts disseminated? Information that accompanies instruction is invaluable. It's material that you'll be able to refer to and use long after the class has ended.

Is there homework? – Experienced teachers will give you scripts to prepare between classes, to keep your skills sharpened and ready for your in-class performances.

Is the business of voice acting addressed? – Techniques are important, acting skills vital, but voice acting is also a business. If you're serious about making voice acting a career, topics specifically related to the business of voice acting should be covered at least at an Advanced level.

Can you audit a class? – It's great to be able to observe a class in action to get a taste of the instructor's teaching style, the topics covered and the place where it's held. You'd be able to follow along and take notes (and ask the occasional question), but don't expect to participate. Mic time is reserved for students who've paid for the course.

Can you make up classes missed? – Some courses allow this, others don't. It's always best to ask the instructor what their policy is.

Do students like the course? – What's the word-of-mouth about the course? Are there testimonials available? Can you contact current or former students directly? Sometimes talking to people who've taken the course can give you a more objective view.

Is there a course assessment? – Do you get any kind of an assessment when you've completed the course? Do you receive a critique that gives you an analysis of your competency or proficiency? It's good to know where you stand, competition-wise, in a very competitive business.

Hopefully, asking these questions should help you figure out the best voice acting class for you. Break a lip!

DEALING WITH DIRECTORS

As a director, I've worked with many diverse voice actors, and as a voice actor, with many different directors. For those of you who are just breaking in to V-O, it's good to know ahead of time what to expect in an actual, paid session. And for those of you who've been doing V-O for years, you'll see that the reason you've been working is because you've been doing the following for so long:

1) Pay close attention to the director after every take. Whatever they ask you to do, mark your copy accordingly and write notes in the margin, even emoticons if necessary.

2) If a director's directions are confusing, politely ask them to clarify. If you're still not understanding them, as a last resort, ask them for a line read: "How do *you* hear it?" Listen carefully to their "notes" and mimic exactly what they say—out loud, so they can hear your emphases and approve it.

3) If there's more than one director in the room, and you're getting conflicting direction, aim your questions at the person who hired you. If they're not there, try to discern who the boss is and aim your questions at them.

4) If you're ever in a situation where the director is verbally abusing you (it's rare, but it happens), stop what you're doing and

ask for short break. Then decide how you're going to tell them that you will not be spoken to that way. No one should tolerate verbal abuse in a professional setting. Stand up for yourself and speak up.

5) Write down the name(s) of everyone involved in the session and thank them individually when you're done, including the engineer.

12 TOP V-O SKILLS

If a dollar dropped out of the sky every time someone asked me what it takes to make it in the world of voiceover, I could retire! But here's what it takes: a dozen top skills that are fundamental to a successful career (i.e., getting lots of repeat work!) in voice acting. And amazingly, they all start with the letter "C"!

1) Clarity – A voice actor's articulation has got to be impeccable. Each word needs to be distinctly understood, not swallowed, mumbled or garbled. An actor needs to make sure that they're balancing their enunciation between over-articulation and under-articulation. We don't want to over-enunciate, or we won't sound conversational—we'll just sound pompous. And we don't want to under-articulate or we'll sound stupid or lazy or both. We need to find the "Goldilocks" area of vocal clarity: not too much, not too little. Employers are always listening for narrators who can speak clearly, without overdoing it or underdoing it. It has to be just right.

2) Cleanliness – This only partly means you should shower before a session. Cleanliness refers to mouth noise, and if you have a lot of it, you may have a difficult time getting work in voiceover. Some people are blessed with minimal mouth noise— they've just inherited a genetic gift that makes their saliva (or lack of it) a non-issue. But most narrators have some level of mouth

noise: those glottal stops, clicks and smacking sounds—that they mitigate a number of ways: hydrating (otherwise known as drinking a lot of water); using throat sprays, mouthwashes or herbal teas; munching tiny pieces of green apple (in between narration excerpts), chewing gum or sucking on a lozenge. But the best way to mitigate mouth noise is simply to breathe through your words and phrases. The less time an editor needs to clean up your V-O tracks, the more chance you'll be called back to do another session. Soon.

3) Consistency – In voiceover, consistency is a highly-valued skill. If you're consistent in your volume, energy, pacing, articulation, characterization and your eye-brain-mouth coordination, you'll be every director's dream, because you'll be a voice actor they can rely on to deliver what they want every time.

4) Connected – Being connected to what you're reading is vital to your performance and the believability of your interpretation. A professional narrator always sounds like they're intrinsically interested in what they're talking about, regardless of whether they are. I always pose the question: if you're not enthusiastic about what you're talking about, why should the listener be interested in what you have to say? Being connected also means being physically connected to the page, with your eyes scanning ahead to make sure you're moving through the copy or text without tripping or stumbling. Voice actors use a number of different techniques to stay connected: using their hands to make points or gestures; inflecting when and where appropriate; making facial expressions to convey emotion and using their body to physically interpret action into their voice.

5) Conversational – Being conversational in voiceover isn't as easy as it sounds. It takes a practiced ability to lift words off the page effortlessly, as if you're speaking extemporaneously (because you're an expert, right?). It means reading (and speaking) at conversational

speed—the typical pace that we speak in everyday conversations. This skill is partly a matter of not over- or under-articulating, and is key to engaging the listener and maintaining their attention.

6) Cold Reading – This skill is a must-have for long-form narration, particularly in the areas of e-Learning modules, instructional CD-Rom narration, and non-fiction audiobooks. If you're a busy voice actor, you don't have time to pre-read dozens or hundreds of pages of text before you take on a project. The ability to cold read text will save you a lot of time in the studio, not to mention a lot of editing time. The ability to scan ahead, to make sense of run-on sentences, and to navigate incorrect punctuation is a skill that comes in very handy. Solid cold reading is the manifestation of excellent eye-brain-mouth coordination, and can be strengthened every day by constant practice. Reading aloud (to your kids, significant other, parent, dog, cat, bird or bunny) will help you become a great cold reader.

7) Chop Chop – Okay, this was my lame "C" phrase for being quick (I could have written "Cwick", but that would've been much lamer). Speaking fast is, in many situations, as essential skill in V-O. It becomes readily apparent in a commercial, where sometimes you're supposed to squeeze 40-seconds of copy into a 30-second time frame (I call this "shoe-horning"). The ability to get through copy rapidly, but not at the expense of clarity, is a crucial skill that, if you haven't mastered, you need to develop.

8) Coordination – I referred to this under Consistency and Cold Reading. This is the mental muscle memory that develops when your eyes take in the words on the page, make the connections in your brain and come out of your mouth. I call it "eye-brain-mouth coordination," and it's a skill that voice actors develop after voicing thousands of pages of copy or text over a number of years. Some people are better at it than others, sometimes reading thousands of words in multiple pages of copy before making a mistake. Developing strong E-B-M coordination is possible by

cold reading copy every day. It's like a musician who practices their scales daily—they strengthen their muscle memory; or it's like going to the gym every other day to build up your muscles and your stamina. Great E-B-M coordination is one of the hallmarks of a professional voice actor.

9) Characterization – Any kind of voice work that requires characterization requires acting, and actors understand what goes into giving a solid performance. Many of the skills I mentioned earlier—consistency, conversationality, being connected—in addition to the acting skills of believability, authenticity, emotionality and interpretation—are immensely important in telling a compelling story. The ability to perform solid characters is another arrow in your quiver of voice acting skills.

10) Convincing – I've heard it said, "Always sound like you know what you're talking about, even if you don't." This could be the mantra for narration. No matter what subject you're talking about, the ability to sound convincing encompasses skills of coherent explanation, a measured, neutral (or sometimes friendly) tone, an appropriate amount of conversationality and energy, and an authoritativeness that's believable and approachable. The most convincing narrators are those who, in Penny Abshire's term, tell, don't sell.

11) Control – Successful voice actors are always in control—of their voice, that is. They can control their pitch, their volume and their breath. They control their pitch by understanding intonation—realizing that there are many musical applications to the spoken word. They control their volume by understanding that volume, for the most part, has to be consistent—it's their intensity that varies throughout a read. They maintain excellent breath control by constantly replenishing the amount of air they need in order to get through words and phrases competently. And they put all of these skills to use when they need to do any pickup

phrases or insertions, so they can match what they've recorded before.

12) Confidence – The best thing you can bring to any V-O session is confidence—true confidence, not a false sense of bravado. Confidence comes from being prepared; understanding the subject, and anticipating the dynamics of the studio session between the actor, director and engineer (and many times, the presence of the client, either in person or on the phone); you can hear confidence in an actor's voice—in their phrasing, presence, and overall performance. Confidence gives you stamina and believability, and makes it easier to work with a director, who may sometimes give you conflicting direction. Confidence also gives you patience, which can really come in handy in many a recording session. I can add three additional "C's" under the heading of confidence: being calm, cool and collected.

There are many more skills that we bring to a session that makes for a successful performance, and so many more attributes that you need to make it in the world of voiceover. But, if you can infuse these dozen major skills into every V-O session, you'll be well on your way to a satisfying and lucrative career in voice acting.

V-O DEMO DOs AND DON'Ts

There are many things to consider and remember before plunging into the project that will be your virtual calling card, help you find an agent, introduce you to casting directors and producers, and help get you work—providing you've achieved competence in voice acting. Here are a few tips to insure a successful outcome:

<u>DO:</u>

- Find an affordable digital studio (with a good SFX and music library) with an engineer and/or director/producer who has a good reputation for creating and directing voiceover talent and demos.

- Make sure to record enough material to cover at least 60 seconds in length. Pick material that shows your range, is nationally branded, and is somewhat current and commercial, i.e., categories that are on the air all the time, like department stores, automotive, banking, etc. Make sure you have only commercial elements on your commercial demo—not promos, trailers, narrations or anything else that could be construed as anything other than a commercial. Use between 5-15 second segments, no longer. And make sure you mention the name of the product or service in your V-O excerpts.

- Some actors actually record parts of their demo in different studios. The theory behind this is that your performances will vary, giving you a slightly different sound. If that's not possible budget-wise, have the engineer put varied amounts of *equalization (EQ)* on your segments. This will make it sound like you've recorded different spots at different studios. But don't obsess over these production techniques. Agents/clients are listening to your voiceprint and performance a bit more than the production values.

- Make sure that your demo shows off your signature voice or your *money voice*, so listeners can get a really good idea what you sound like. Your demo should showcase various *shades* of you, not different character voices. Save those for your animation demo.

- Select Radio or TV copy that shows some range, and pick copy for products and services that match your age, i.e., young people shouldn't be doing products and services for much older people and vice versa. And don't string together a bunch of tag lines—it doesn't showcase your acting abilities. It's much easier to sell something you believe in than something you don't. Using copy from magazines is iffy—that copy was written for print, not broadcast. But if you're a good copywriter, you can adapt some print copy for your demo.

- If it's just you and the engineer, make sure you have duplicate scripts for him or her. If you're working with a demo producer/ director, they'll have scripts for everyone involved.

- Prepare. *Pre-production* is key. Have your spot excerpts/ scripts rehearsed and timed out. Unless music is being cast for you, have an idea of what music you'd like behind specific pieces, and have a list of SFX you'd like to try. Make sure you get a good night's rest, have something to eat (avoid dairy, carbonated drinks, spicy, greasy, fried or salty foods, liquor and cigarettes) about two hours before the session, and bring plenty of water. It'll be one of the most exhausting sessions you'll ever experience!

- If you can afford it, get an experienced V-O demo director/ producer to help you. It's very difficult to be objective about something as subjective as the sound of your own voice, or the believability of your own performance. I've enlisted the aid of some of my colleagues to help me craft some of my own V-O demos.

- Sequence. Sequencing is crucial. If segments are similar, break them up with ones that are different (e.g., voice alone, voice with music, voice with SFX, dialogue, etc.). They should include reads that are up-tempo/retail, sexy/romantic, serious, straight, real character, compassionate, anything humorous, etc.

- Allow sound effects and music to add variety, but not always on every excerpt.

- Start with your strongest material. You never know how long someone is going to listen to your demo.

- Keep your edits crisp and hard, your fades short. One technique I've heard is splicing non sequiturs together—they add levity and interest. For example, one audio snippet might say, "I love my mom." And the next would say, "That's why I fill her up with the best quality gasoline." Together, they sound funny.

- Everyone says to limit your demo to one minute—agents don't like them any longer. But I say to shoot for 70-80 seconds and let your potential agent decide which excerpts they like best, to cut it down to 60 seconds. This way, you know that they're critically listening to your demo.

- If your demo is in CD format, print your cell phone number somewhere on your demo so producers and casting directors can get in touch with you immediately, as well as your email address and a website, if you have one. If you have an agent, make sure you print their name and number as well. And always include your contact number on all outgoing emails.

- If you're in L.A. or New York City, get the Voice-Over Resource Guide (VORG) to find a list of demo producers to help you produce your new demo, graphics companies to help you design and package your demo, and talent agencies and casting companies to submit your demo to. Ask your teachers and other people in the business for their recommendations, and then shop around if you wish. And don't duplicate hundreds of CDs. Burn one-offs as you need them. Nowadays, though, you rarely need a physical CD. Most of the time you can either attached an .mp3 file of your demo or send a potential client an active link to your website or landing page.

DON'T:

- Make a demo until you've developed all the necessary skills to enter and successfully complete a voiceover session. Bottom line: *you need to be as good as your demo*—your demo shouldn't exceed your abilities. Whatever types of reads you put on your demo you should be able to perform flawlessly at a session. Unless you're pre-pared to walk into a studio with the confidence to read and deliver a piece of copy to five people in the control room and another five people phone-patched in from another city, you're not ready. I know of too many instances where actors were booked off their demo, but couldn't perform anywhere near that quality in the actual session. To reiterate: *don't do a demo until you're really ready*.

- Do impressions on your commercial demo. Most advertisers that want a celebrity voice book the celebrity. But if you're really good at impressions, put them in a separate Character Demo (along with other voices).

- Make a homemade demo—unless you have a super professional setup and know what you're doing in production. If not, it sounds cheap and amateurish, and no one will hire you based on that sound. If you want to make a rough demo for your ears only in order to hear the flow of the segments, fine.

- Record a dialogue segment with a person who's the same sex. If you're a woman, perform your dialogue segment with a man, and vice versa, and make sure you have the lion's share of dialogue. The exception to this rule: if you perform the segment with a child or a much older-sounding person.

- Write your own copy—unless you can write as well as or better than professional copywriters. A good demo producer will have many samples of some recent copy for you to pick from and work with.

- Try to perform copy that's way outside your range. For instance, don't try to mimic a deep, intoning announcer if you don't have the pipes or resonance—you just won't sound convincing—to be competitive.

- Try to fake older if you have a young sound. Conversely, if you have a mature sound, don't try to sound like a kid—you just won't sound believable—unless you're trying out for an animated character. That said, there are a number of women—and a few men—who've got a great facility at sounding much younger than they actually are.

- Spend your life savings on your demo. If you can't afford to do it right, wait until you've saved up enough money. And nowadays you can design your own website for a virtual pittance until you can spring for something more fancy down the road.

- Send out your CD (if you have to send one out) in an ultra-thin case or envelope—they have no spines! Your CD will be invisible to anyone who's storing it. Make sure your name is as big as it can be, and stands out against the background. But most voice actors now send an active link to their website or landing page or attach their demo in an email.

There's an old expression I'm sure you've heard before: "Do it right, or don't do it at all." Remember, you usually only get one chance to make an impression in this business, so make sure your demo is the best it can be!

FINDING A QUALIFIED
V-O COACH

Many of these questions are similar to the guidelines of finding a great voice acting class, but here's a list of questions to ask a potential voiceover coach to determine whether they're up to snuff:

How experienced are you? - Is the V-O coach a voice actor, casting director or producer? If so, they'll know the latest trends in what clients are listening for in auditions.

What's the basic setup? - You need to hear the feedback and information between takes recorded for your subsequent review. Make sure that no matter whom you train with, that you get a digital recording of your performance, along with their critiques on the same audio file. That way you can listen back to how you did in the session and hear whether you made progress.

Do you work with anyone, regardless of experience? – Good coaches screen prospective students to make sure that they've got the basic skills necessary to get the most out their training. They quickly vet potential students to evaluate their experience and skills, and ask what they expect to get out of coaching. And if a person has challenges like dyslexia or speech or breathing problems, they refer them to a specialist.

Do materials accompany instruction? – Are ancillary articles included in coaching sessions? Information that accompanies instruction is invaluable. It's material that you'll be able to refer to and use long after the class has ended.

Is there homework? – Professional V-O coaches will give you homework to prepare between sessions to expose you to many different V-O genres and delivery styles.

Can you re-schedule a session in an emergency? – Some coaches charge you if you have to cancel a session at the last minute, others don't. Always ask.

Do students like the coach? - What's the word-of-mouth? Are there testimonials available? Can you contact current or former students directly? Sometimes talking to people who've taken the course can give you a more objective view.

What are the hourly rates? - Rates vary from as low as $50/hr. to as high as $250/hr. Some offer discounts for multiple sessions.

Hopefully, by asking these questions, you'll be able to find the best voiceover coach. Break a lip!

A PERSPECTIVE ON BOOKING

I f you haven't been booking work for a while, it may not necessarily mean that you're doing something wrong.

I've worked with a lot of professional talent who complain
that they haven't been booking anywhere near what they've been
doing in the past. If this sounds like you, consider this perspective:

1) Today, more than ever, it's a numbers game. There are more
people involved in voiceover these days—a lot more. The advent
of the pay-to-play websites gave voice work much more visibility,
and made the field a lot more competitive. The average number
of actors who auditioned for one job twenty years ago used to be
about 75-100. Now it's about 150-200. Some clients listen only to
the first 10 or 20 auditions, but you'd be surprised at how many clients listen to all submissions in hopes of finding that perfect voice.
Do they listen all the way through the audition? Most times, no. If
they don't hear anything they like in the first five or ten seconds,
they move on to the next audition. Which brings me to...

2) You could be doing everything right in your audition: good
articulation, great performance, and good production values.
But if you're not the voice that the client hears in their head, you
won't be picked. Keep in mind: you could be the best actor in the
world, but if the client doesn't think your voiceprint is the best

match for their product or service, you won't get the gig, even if you have a voice that makes James Earl Jones sound like a frog. Which brings me to...

3) When you submit an audition from your agent, you're competing against a lot of other talented actors. Some agencies will contact at least five to ten talent agencies, plus some independent casting services. If agencies submit just their top ten talent, that adds up to a lot of people, and a LOT of competition. But when you submit an audition to a pay-to-play site, honestly, as a producer who's posted jobs there occasionally, odds are about 75% of those performances will not be as competitive. So if you're a pro talent, you'll actually be competing only against 25% of auditioners.

4) Once you submit an audition, don't expect anyone to acknowledge it. Send it and forget about it, and move on to the next one.

POSITIVES AND NEGATIVES

W e're all familiar with positives and negatives: in math; on a magnet, on a battery; protons and electrons; yin and yang.

Well, there are also positives and negatives in voice acting. And recognizing them is easy, because we speak in positives and negatives all the time in our everyday conversations. And we do it unconsciously.

The concept is simple. Positive words sound positive. Words like love, peace and hope are positive, imbued with goodness. They're words/ideas we aspire to. They're *uplifting* words/concepts, and we unconsciously lift those words when we say them. But words like hate, murder and racism are negative, imbued with badness. These words we unconsciously *push down*, giving them a negative tone. So we lift our voices on positive words, and do the opposite with negatives—we push them down.

Think of it this way: when you refer to positive things, you're saying, "I approve—thumbs up." When you utter negative concepts your voice says, "I disapprove—thumbs down."

So it all boils down to the *sound of good and bad*. Ever hear the lyrics "Accentuate the positive, eliminate the negative"? Well, in copy, we can easily accentuate the positive, but we can't eliminate the negative. We have to treat the negative the opposite way we treat the positive.

It's a simple equation: lift the positive, push down the negative. You can hear it in two words: "good" and "bad." When you lift "good" (with a smile) it sounds good. When you push down "bad" (with a frown) it sounds bad. Try reversing it. Lift bad with a smile. Sounds odd, doesn't it? And the reverse: pushing down on "good" sounds strange. It has an odd ring.

But the proof of the pudding is in the tasting. What happens when positive and negative words are turned upside down? For instance, the word "good" in and of itself, is a positive word. "Oh, that's really good!" said sincerely, calls for you to naturally lift the word. But couched in sarcasm, in negativity, you'd take that same phrase and make "good" sound derisive: "Oh, *that's* really good" (accompanied by an eye roll).

Now take the word "bad." In and of itself, it's negative: "That's bad!" Not a good thing. You push the last word down, indicating you don't approve. But have you ever heard a little kid get excited about a game or toy or whatever and hear him or her say, "Ooh, that's bad!" as in, "Ooh, that's good!"? They lift the last word, imbuing it with goodness, smiling, basically saying "This is cool!"

And when I say lift, it doesn't need to be a huge lift. It needs to be subtle. Gentle. Nuanced. This goes especially for commercial copy, where you're expected to billboard the name of the advertiser and stress the copy points or benefits of the product or service.

Positives and negatives abound in copy and text. The obvious words and phrases are adjectives, but they can also be verbs, adverbs, even nouns, so you've got an opportunity to infuse them with the appropriate positive and negative tones they convey, to give more depth to the stories you're telling.

TELEPHONE ETIQUETTE

Some of your work as a voice actor will not be performing—it'll be working the telephone. Since your first voice audition for a potential employer could be over the phone, it's <u>critical</u> that your phone etiquette is professional and polished. I can't stress enough how important it is to make a good first impression on the phone—it's one of the most fundamental tools you'll need to develop for whatever work you do. Here are some simple guidelines to keep in mind:

- *Find the person you want to reach.* Make friends with receptionists. They're the gate keepers, and you don't want to annoy them. If your contact person isn't available, leave a concise message on their voice-mail.

- *Have a calm, quiet background.* Make sure there's no noise behind you while you're on the phone. No TV, no barking dogs or screeching birds, no crying babies or screaming kids, no gardeners blowing or vacuum cleaners sucking, no office sounds or other phones ringing. Either simple music or nothing at all.

- *Have a good phone service.* Make sure your phone has good fidelity and make sure you never miss a call. Get a call-waiting feature that rolls over any incoming calls to your outgoing message. Make your outgoing message clear, concise and informative—you can even mention that you're not available because you're probably in a session—with instructions for numbers to call for voice messages and pages. If you have to leave a message, decide on what you're going to say before you say it, so you don't get tongue-tied.

- *Manners matter.* If you're on the phone with a prospective employer, don't put them on hold. Besides being rude, it shows that you have no respect for their time and interrupts the purpose of your call.

- *Write down what you're going to say.* Have this script in front of you as you speak. You may memorize it after a while, but always refer to it to keep it fresh.

- *Who, What, Why, If, How and When.* Once you've connected with the person you want to talk to, introduce yourself and tell them why you're calling, and if and how (email, CD, etc.) you can submit your V-O demo.

- *Verify, Verify, Verify.* Verify the spelling of a business contact's name, title, the spelling of their company name, and their address. Don't assume you know the spelling of *anyone's* name, even John (it could be Jon, Geon, Jonn, etc.) Get their email address right so you can add them to your database.

- *Keep it brief.* You've got 10-15 seconds—max—to say what you're going to say. These are very busy people you're talking to, so get to the point quickly.

- *Be unfailingly polite, have good energy and a smile.* Calling scores of people over and over can wear you down after a while. After an hour on the phone, stretch, take a break, and get back to it with renewed vigor.

- *Project your voice and articulate.* You're a voice actor—act like one! Speak clearly, intelligently and concisely. Be yourself, but don't goof around with a faux DJ voice, or try out your character voices on a business call. This isn't a performing audition. Be professional. Friendly, but professional.

- *Be conversational.* If your contact asks you questions about yourself, be forthcoming, but keep it brief. If they give you an opening, ask about them—if they like what they do, how they got into the business, etc. People love to talk about themselves. The more info they give you, the more you have to talk to them about the next time you speak to them.

- *Keep records.* Whatever your system—maintain a record of conversations you have with each and every person you call.

- *Follow up.* There's no point in going through the motions of contacting prospective employers and sending them your demo (or to your demo) if you don't follow up. Ask your contact what their procedure is—then ask *when* would be a good time to contact them again. Be diligent, but don't be a pest.

- *Answer your phone professionally.* You never know who's calling. A simple, "Hi, this is Joan" is fine—unless your name's Harry. Thank all business contacts for returning your call and get right to business.

- *Be available 18/7.* As an actor, you have to always be connected—you never know when someone might need you to audition *within the next hour!* If your cellphone rings and it's a potential client, get to a quiet place immediately. Check your messages occasionally. If you find you're missing messages, get a reliable service.

Your phone script helps you from getting tongue-tied or distracted. Keep it short, sweet and to the point. In some instances, consider standing when you're talking—you sound authoritative and confident. Your phone call is like an audition. But it's also a mini-job interview. At the end of the conversation, ask them *how* you can send your demo, not if. Don't give them the chance to say no.

You have to *use* your voice to *sell* your voice, and you can't sell a product if you can't sell your voice. If you're new in town, tell them. If you've just snagged a major campaign that's on the air, make a point of mentioning it.

Always be unfailingly polite, and if the situation calls for it, joke a bit—you can usually tell whether or not the person at the other end has a sense of humor. Move the conversation along briskly, understanding that the person you're talking to doesn't have a lot of time to gab. Don't forget to thank them for their time and information. But if, for whatever reason, the person you're talking to is rude, take the higher road and just say something like, "It seems like you're having a bad day. I'll call back at a better time," and hang up. Write the incident in your records and call back in a couple of months to see if that person may have moved on.

10 CRUCIAL SKILLS FOR AUDIOBOOK NARRATION

Narrating an audiobook is the most challenging work you can do in voiceover. It takes a lot of skill to navigate them successfully. I'm wont to say that if a 30-second spot is like running a 50-yard dash and a 60-second spot is like a 100-yard dash, an audiobook is like running a 26.2K marathon. If you can master the ten skills below, you'll be successful in accomplishing a performance that audiobook aficionados appreciate.

1 – Articulation: This involves enunciating words and phrases correctly, clearly and cleanly; there should be no over- or under-articulation (unless it's a character); there should be no sibilance or whistling (most commonly heard on "s's" or soft "c's") or lisping, and little to no mouth noise.

2 – Breathing: You must have enough breath so that you don't run out of air at the end of sentences, or grasp for breath in between sentences or inside them. There should be no fading, swallowing or gulping. Breath control also involves controlling plosives (popping p's or hard consonants), keeping your volume consistent and projection appropriate. Manage mouth noise and throat clearing. Too much will require a lot of editing, and subsequently, audiobook companies will not hire talent who engender a lot of post-production attention.

3 – Delivery: The ability to tell a story compellingly is what constitutes solid delivery. Your delivery must be appropriate to the spirit of the text and the author's intent, and must be consistent throughout the narration. As you'll most likely be narrating over several days, your voice must match itself from day to day, pitch-wise and energy-wise. Timing and pacing are additional elements of professional delivery, and needs to be appropriate to the text. Repetitive cadence and pitch patterns in narration must be avoided at all costs. Each sentence needs to be varied slightly, so as not to become predictable. Listeners may not know *what* you're going to say next, but if you're constantly starting and ending sentences the same way all the time, they'll know *how* you're going to say what you're going to say. Listening to yourself, remembering what you did, listening to your director (if you have one) and making adjustments are other must-have delivery skills.

4 – Eye-Brain-Mouth Control: This skill involves reading the script accurately; not omitting, adding or changing any words/ phrases (unless it's an obvious typo). Minimizing your mistakes is important: the more you make, the longer it'll take you to narrate the book and the less money you'll make per finished hour. Lifting words off the page without a lot of mistakes takes practice but can make you a decent amount of money.

5 – Consistency: Ralph Waldo Emerson wrote, "A foolish consistency is the hobgoblin of little minds." But consistency is highly prized in audiobook narration. Consistent energy, articulation, breath control, pitch control and characterization will get a narrator hired repeatedly, because audiobook publishers can count on them to deliver.

6 – Analysis/Interpretation: This requires understanding the story arc and the characters (in fiction), discerning your listening audience, and employing the appropriate delivery. It involves understanding concepts and making them understandable to the listener.

7 – Characterization: Bringing life—and a sound—to your characters is a must. They must be distinct from each other and consistent in their tone, attitude, age and accent. Their voices much match their given character description (if there is any), so the more character voices you have in your vocal bag of tricks, the better.

8 – Separation: This skill means no "spillover" between narrator and character. Make sure that phrases like "he said" or "she said" before or after a character speaks—is in the narrator's voice, not the character's.

9 – Stamina: An audiobook narrator spends approximately four to six hours behind a microphone per day. This requires unflagging energy, and the ability to sound as strong at the end of the day as the beginning. Narrators who are physically fit and emotionally stable will be able to muster the stamina necessary to sustain a professional narration.

10 – Investment: You need to "invested" in what you're talking about—interested, connected to the story. Being sincerely interested in your subject matter—even if it's boring—draws the listener in, garners great reviews, and motivates an audiobook publisher to hire you again.

TIPS FOR SOUNDING LIKE A "REAL PERSON"

How many times have you read these directions for a V-O script? "Non-actors, please! Real people needed, not voiceovers!" Sounding like a real person is one of the hardest things to do in voice acting.

Actors are trained to have good articulation and voice actors even more so. So when it comes time to inhabit a "real person" persona, here are a few things to try:

1) *Relax your articulation. Here's a list of phrases that need relaxing and their offspring:*

    going to = gonna
    got to = gotta
    let me = lemme
    kind of = kinda
    sort of = sorta
    little = l'il
    give me = gimme
    want to = wanna
    should have = shoulda

could have = coulda
would have = woulda
who are you = whoareya
what are you = whattaya or whatca
when are you = whenaya
which of you = whichaya
why are you = whyareya
did you = didja or didjoo
would you = wouldja or wouldjoo
what you = wutcha or wutchoo

2) Contract words that need contracting.

Copywriters are somewhat inconsistent with this, so if you see a few contractions in a piece of copy but a number of places that call out for a contraction, contract away, particularly if the direction calls for being real and conversational.

3) Drop the "g" in words ending with "ing."

Comin', goin', doin', seein', bein'...now we're talkin'. We drop our g's all the time in conversation, so when appropriate, drop those g's and sound a bit more real. Know what I'm sayin'?

4) Stammer or stutter.

W-we do this all the time when we're talking. Not a lot, but occasionally. If you find an appropriate place to do it, do it.

5) Repeat words occasionally.

How...how many times to we do this in conversation? More than we think. Find occasional places to add this technique to your read.

6) Stretch your words.

How many times...do we streeeetch our words out? Not a lot, but we do, and you can do it, too. I don't know where I heard the phrase, but someone in our business called it "taffy pulling," and that's a great description. Find an appropriate place to apply that.

7) Grope for words.

Not only do we stretch, we...grope. It's the sound of you thinking. When you think out loud of different possibilities, you hesitate for a fraction of a second. That's the sound of groping for a word.

8) Breathe.

Don't be afraid to breathe when you're talking and try not to edit out breaths during your performance. The more human you are, the better.

9) Don't worry too much about mouth noise.

Just like breaths, leave in the flaws, i.e., mouth noise. You can edit out slurping, however. In fact, don't include any disgusting noises, unless your character calls for that.

10) Use non-verbal sounds between and inside of your words

Almost anything goes for non-verbal sounds. There are innumerable non-verbal sounds that can accompany copy, whether placed in between words or in the words themselves. Sighing into a word or through it is totally appropriate in the sentence, "Boy, am I tired." Chuckling or laughing before or during, "He looked so funny!" sounds much more believable than just saying those words.

11) Vary your cadence.

No one talks in a steady beat. We pause for reflection or to make a point, and your cadence should reflect that. Find places in your copy to take a beat now and then, a dramatic pause. Nobody wants to hear you talking relentlessly. And I never met an actor who didn't love a dramatic beat.

Here's the bottom line for using any of the aforementioned tips: determine if it's appropriate to apply it, and when you do, do it judiciously.

PRACTICING

A few years ago, a student sent me an article about world-renowned musical artists and how they felt about practicing. Every one of them said that they didn't like to practice, but they all did it—in fact, they felt they *had* to practice to stay on top of their game and to keep up with or stay ahead of their competition.

There are many things in the field of voice acting that can be studied—that's knowledge—things you learn abstractly and mentally. But skills—well, those are things you develop as you work on them, or practice. They usually involve some physical coordination, and most times they get easier the more you do them. You can learn about them in books, TV, the Internet, in lectures and classrooms. But you can't learn to apply them unless you practice.

I started piano lessons when I was about seven years old. My piano teacher sat me down and showed me the things I was supposed to practice for the next week: different scales and a short piano piece. He showed me how to sit, where to place my fingers, how to move them and what each exercise and piece should sound like. I was supposed to practice at least thirty minutes each day until the next lesson. And when he showed up the following week, his initial comments were either, "Marc, it sounds like you practiced," or "Marc, it sounds like you didn't practice." Teachers have a way of knowing right away whether you buckled down or slacked off.

I don't know how many times I've had people tell me, "I think I've got a pretty good voice," and then ask, "Do you think I'd be good at voiceover?" And my answer is always the same: You can have the most beautiful-sounding voice in the world, but if you don't know what to do with it, it's useless. You can learn skills, but you'll never realize your full potential unless you practice.

Now, practicing a lot doesn't always mean that you'll get better the more you do it. You could be practicing wrong techniques, doing things incorrectly, practicing bad form and strengthening bad habits. That's why it's so important to work with an experienced instructor, who's mastered the skills you're trying to achieve; who's giving you specific and constructive feedback so you can build a strong foundation of skills while you're learning.

Sometimes the exercises you practice will feel natural and easy when you're starting out; other times they might feel awkward or downright impossible. If you experience the latter, that's okay: you're attempting to do something new, so feeling frustrated or self-conscious about being uncoordinated is normal. But the more you practice, the easier the exercises will become. It's just like learning a musical instrument—it's muscle memory, and you're building up your mental and physical muscles. The more familiar you get with a piece of copy, the more it'll sound natural and conversational, because you begin to internalize it and not struggle with the "mechanics" of speaking the words.

What you practice is crucial. If you have a good instructor, you'll have specific exercises to practice, vocal warm-ups that include articulating all the consonants and vowels, singing, wrestling with tongue-twisters and sibilant words and phrases. These exercises are a great way to develop the necessary eye-brain-mouth coordination needed for all professional voiceover work. They're just like practicing musical scales: they're exercises you need to perform over and over again until they flow effortlessly. And don't rely solely on your teacher to get material to practice. The Internet has a plethora of ad and text copy for you to practice with that you can download for free, and there are many V-O books on the market, with hundreds of different exercises.

How you practice is important. Make sure your diaphragm and lungs can expand easily, that your posture is correct, that you're projecting your voice properly and consistently moving air. An experienced teacher will give you resistance exercises to build up your tongue, mouth and facial muscles. They'll also give you advice on what and what not to eat or drink before warming up. Also, recording yourself is a great way to practice. This way you can critique yourself, finding weak points that you can concentrate and improve on. A reminder: as you listen back to your voice, don't beat yourself up if it's not coming out perfect. We've all heard, "Practice Makes Perfect" too many times. Now, I don't know about perfect, but I definitely know practice makes better. You strive to be your best, you aim for perfection, but perfection is elusive. If you practice to keep getting better, you'll be able, many times, to hit those perfect moments, those times when you're "in the zone," flawlessly executing a voice performance. But if you expect to be absolutely perfect every time you get behind the mic, you're setting yourself up for disappointment.

Where you practice also makes a difference. If you have a home studio (whether simple or elaborate), practice there. It's great when you can kind of re-create the environment where you'll eventually be performing. Practicing your proximity to the microphone, with and without headphones, determining a sitting or standing position, adjusting for line-of-sight (that's where you can see the copy clearly but still be on-mic) and proper lighting—all things that you'll encounter in the real world—are really helpful. The more comfortable you get, the more at ease you'll be in an actual session. If you're serious about voiceover and don't have a home studio yet, look into setting one up. They're very inexpensive now (sometimes under $500).

Getting back to the artists I mentioned at the beginning: remember they said they didn't like practicing, but did it anyway? Well, they found ways to make practicing interesting, challenging and fun. Amy Nathan, author of *Beating Those Practice-Time Blues,* relates that Joshua Bell, world-renowned violinist, said he had plenty of fights about not wanting to practice. Wynton Marsalis didn't always want to play trumpet; he wanted to play basketball. André Watts said he liked playing piano as a kid but didn't always like doing the work.

How did they approach practicing? Joshua Bell said, "I'd set up challenges for myself, like I wouldn't stop until I did a difficult passage a certain number of times in a row without a mistake. By the time I did it that many times, I'd learned it and made a game out of it."

Wynton Marsalis learned how to warm up with his trumpet exercises from playing basketball. He said, "In basketball, you practice your foot movement, your floor game, going to either side, your jump shot, free-throw shooting. It seemed like the intelligent thing to do the same with trumpet, to work on all the different aspects of technique." You can do the same with copy and text. Your practicing should obviously include the pieces you're working on. I send my students scripts to practice *before* they show up for class or one-on-one sessions, and then correct them, if necessary.

Flutist Paula Robison recommends finding a warm-up exercise "that makes you happy. It should be filled with music from the first note, so you warm up that part of your playing, too." So find text passages or ad copy that are interesting and/or entertaining to read out loud. And practice at the volume you'd be speaking in a session, not whispering to yourself.

How do you get inspired to practice each day? Listen! Listen to the voices of people you admire—your favorite audiobook narrator, your favorite documentary narrator, and demos from the top talent on Voices.com. Listen to get inspired, but don't be intimidated. These are people who've practiced for thousands of hours at their craft, and continue to do so to stay on top of their game.

People ask me all the time, "Will I ever be able to be as good as the amazingly talented people I hear?" And I tell them that there's only one way to level the playing field when going up against voice actors with a lot more experience: have great skills. And there's only one way to develop and eventually apply those skills: practice.

TO STAND OR TO SIT?

Does every script require standing up? Your stature affects how you speak. But there's no rule that says you have to stand for everything you read. Sure, if the spot requires a lot of energy, standing is smart, because it allows you to use your whole body to channel the energy you'll need to deliver your copy or lines. But if the copy calls for a thoughtful, quiet read, why stand? Reads like that require what I call an "armchair" delivery, as if you were sitting, relaxed, in a comfy chair in front of a fireplace.

A stool is a great way to sit, yet be upright for a read. It allows your diaphragm to expand, but lets you relax your center of gravity. Some narrators are perfectly comfortable reading at a desk. Just keep in mind that there's not just one way to deliver copy. It all depends on what kind of story you're telling and how active your body needs to be.

Virtually every audiobook narrator sits in a comfortable chair, because they're usually reading for a number of hours. Some sit straight up; others slant their bodies a bit, as if they were sitting in a chaise lounge. If this works for you, consider giving yourself a bit of lower back support, with a small pillow. Sitting in a chair for a long time takes its toll on your neck, back and spine.

UPSPEAK OR UPTALK

Turning statements into questions is quite common these days. It's a way of speaking called upspeak, or uptalk, and it's usually done unconsciously.

It all started with the "Valley Girl" phenomenon in songs and movies in the '80s, where a San Fernando Valley, CA teen would constantly lift the end of a lot of phrases: "So he said I'm crazy? for doing that? but I do it all the time? and nobody says anything?" Soon it became known as California Upspeak, then spread across the country and eventually around the world, so now you hear it virtually everywhere you go.

Have you ever asked someone their name and they answer you with what sounds like a question? "My name's Mary?" That's upspeak, but it's a lot more pervasive, and it's really unconscious. Most people who upspeak don't even hear it when they're doing it. And if you listen carefully to ads or virtually any form of recorded speech, you'll hear it a lot.

I hear upspeak creeping into a lot of ads these days, and while occasionally appropriate, I believe that if you're a spokesperson, you need to be careful about getting into any kind of upspeak. Upspeak undermines your authority. When you put a question mark after the name of the product or its benefits, you become the voice of "I'm not sure." When upspeak pervades your story, some listeners will wonder if you know what you're talking about. If you're a spokesperson, you need to sound sure of what you're saying.

Now, I'm not saying that upspeak is a no-no. Upspeak is now part of our way of vernacular and is contemporary (but maddening). It has its place, sometimes when you're telling a story in the first person. "So I ran into Barbara the other day and she looked fabulous, dropped 40 pounds and ditched her loser boyfriend!" Upspeak would put the sound of a question mark on *Barbara, day, fabulous* and *pounds*, but not on *boyfriend*.

Be cognizant of your upspeak. Listen to yourself and critically listen to how often (or not) you employ it. You should be able to hear it and control it, applying it when you want to. If you decide it's appropriate to use, be judicious—don't be using it willy-nilly, unless it's a character that uses it all the time. Control your upspeak. Don't let it control you.

DO YOU HAVE AN EDGE
IN VOICE ACTING?

S tage, TV and film actors, as well as singers, instructors, public speakers and on-air talent ask me questions all the time about whether they might have a shot at voice acting, or voiceover—especially when the number of voice acting opportunities is growing every year. Commercials, narrations, animation, promos, trailers, audiobooks, video games, voice-mail systems, e-Learning modules, corporate videos, interactive CD-ROMS, telephone interactive voice recordings (IVRs), website narrations and much more are being produced worldwide every day, due to the advancements and growth of media technology.

If you're in one of the aforementioned fields and you've ever considered exploring the arena of voice acting, you may have an edge or a leg up in this industry. It depends on the amount and/ or type of experience you've had in your particular field. If you inhabit any of the aforementioned areas of using your voice for a living, here are some of the skill-sets that you've probably developed that you can use to your advantage in voice acting:

Stage actors: Stage actors have developed a great ability to "lift" lines. In rehearsal, they'll usually hold the script in one hand, glance at their lines and then deliver them without looking at the page. They also have good articulation, because their words have to be understood by a live audience. Their performances call for a lot of physicality, which they use to enhance their character. Stage actors are also talented at improvisation, are more spontaneous and freer with their emotions, and can quickly tap into them. These abilities are very helpful for voice actors in commercials and animation, as it prepares them for producers who'll tell them what emotion(s) they want exhibited in a script, and encourages them to improvise beyond just the words on the page.

But, voice acting is based upon using your normal voice. Many stage actors are taught to project so that their voice can be heard in the back of the theater, without the need for a microphone. Also, being in front of a live audience assumes the audience can see them, whereas no one can see you behind a microphone, which calls for a much more nuanced read. A voice actor knows that a microphone needs to be treated as if they're talking into someone's ear, talking to one person or a few persons—rarely to an audience. When you listen to a documentary, a voice-menu-prompt system, or even a national television commercial, you'll tend to hear a more natural-style voice delivery. V-O directors typically search for voice actors who can use their natural voices behind the microphone, and rarely want any theatricality. Once stage actors understand the difference in dynamics between live theater and a small recording booth, they can easily make the transition into voice acting, particularly in commercial and animation work.

TV and Film actors: Film actors also have an edge because of their ability to lift their lines as well, eventually memorizing their lines and internalizing their emotions and attitudes. The sensitive microphones used in film making today can capture a whisper, and an actor's nuanced soliloquy caught on camera is very adaptable to voice work. They're able to "say" things without saying a word through their facial expressions and/or body language, so that it seems to the viewer that they've "become" their character. They're able to take direction and also offer up suggestions to the director if asked. They're usually prepared for their performance, memorizing their lines and deciding what they're going to do physically to enhance their role.

While on-camera actors expressing emotions without saying a word is very powerful on screen, voice acting is a different medium—it requires actors to emote without being seen. They need to learn how to express emotion and attitude through words alone—no one can see their face or body language. And they have to learn to express themselves non-verbally as well, sometimes communicating without uttering actual words, but sounds. But, like stage actors, they've developed a way to access emotions quickly and believably, and this puts them in good stead to be potential voice actors.

Singers: Singers bring a wealth of skill-sets to voice acting. They understand the fundamentals of articulation, projection, phrasing and interpretation. As performers with a keen sense of musicality, they have a nice range and their intonation is solid, with perfect relative pitch or sometimes perfect pitch. They also have excellent breath control and microphone technique.

What singers quickly realize when they're working in voiceover is the amount of "music" there is in copy. They hear the different keys that voice actors can speak in, the fluidity and tempo in the cadence of speech. They realize that there's the same kind of colorization and interpretation of words and phrasing in lifting words off the page that occurs in singing a song, and that the effort of delivering a great musical performance on stage or in a studio is just as difficult for a narration. Their innate musicality gives them a keen insight into hearing the "music" of copy or text. Another skill singers bring is what my friend and colleague Robin Armstrong calls "tonal memory"—the ability to consistently remember the intonation of copy.

Instructors: Good instructors have a great way of getting concepts across in an intelligible way, and never talk down to their students. They're able to grasp the big picture of an idea or ideas and make sense of things to the unenlightened. They're able to take their students one step at a time through a series of facts and string them together so they're understandable. And they're able to articulate all of these elements with enthusiasm that keeps the listener engaged and, hopefully, inspired.

Voice actors do the exact same things when they're telling a story. When they're performing fiction especially, they bring all their acting skills to the fore. However, narrators who are not great actors, but have good articulation and interpretation, are great candidates for non-fiction material (any non-fiction audio-book, explainer video narrations, e-Learning modules, website narrations, guided tours, children's instructional videogames, telephone messaging, etc.). So an instructor who speaks clearly and intelligently, even though they're not an actor, has a good chance of being competitive in voiceover, particularly in the non-fiction areas.

Public speakers: Professional public speakers bring together the attributes of stage actors and instructors. They're comfortable and enthusiastic talking about their subject matter, and many use physicality in their performances to enhance their message. They also have solid microphone technique, whether they're using a headset or standing behind a podium. They have a great sense of timing, pacing and humor, and are usually very articulate.

Public speakers who are thinking of transitioning into voice acting need to realize that in a studio, they're talking to just one or a few persons, not an entire audience; that they're not making a speech, but telling a story; that they have no props or PowerPoint programs to fall back on—just the words that come out of their mouths. So they're going from a stage and spotlight and large audience (like stage actors) to a small booth and a microphone, with an audience of one or two (the director and the engineer) or none (if they're recording in their home studio—alone). If they don't mind this sea change, they, too, have a decent shot at participating in voice acting.

On-air talent: Radio DJ's, hosts and personalities have a lot of skill-sets that many people in the voice-over world don't appreciate. They have excellent eye-brain-mouth coordination, i.e., they're able to lift words off a page effortlessly, without stumbling over any words, rarely omitting or adding any, and giving them the appropriate energy. They're also able to speak very quickly, with outstanding articulation—an amazing ability to "shoe-horn" seventy seconds of copy into a sixty-second spot. They have exceptional cold-reading ability, since many of them come from the "rip and read" school of "This just in!" on-air announcing (the phrase "rip and read" came from the phenomenon of in the early days of Radio where broadcasters, delivering the news live, would rip the paper coming off a machine called a teletype—the forerunner of the fax machine—and read it—cold—to listeners). On-air personalities are able to ad-lib extremely well, particularly in testimonials, giving advertisers a lot of bang for their buck. But most incredibly of all, they're able to do all these things *live*, with thousands, hundreds of thousands or possibly millions of people listening to them. That's a heck of a lot of pressure on a person, something that most professional voice actors rarely, if ever, encounter. In any given V-O session, you'll have an audience of just a few people maximum hanging on your every word.

Unfortunately, many radio DJs, announcers or personalities wear headphones while they're on the air, and have basically fallen in love with the purring, resonant sound of their own voices. Most have been inculcated by their program director to deliver station-written and produced copy in the same style that they use on the air, because that's what the advertiser wants and is paying for.

Many on-air talents have listened to their predecessors for years, and have consciously or unconsciously emulated their sometimes unctuous, sometimes in your face, sometimes over-the-top style. But I've worked with a number of former on-air talent who've successfully made the transition to voice acting. It just takes some training.

Now, if you aren't in the above-mentioned categories, it doesn't mean that you don't have a shot at voice acting. But the skills that people in these areas possess are skills that they've honed for thousands of hours and years of experience, and can be applied to a potentially successful V-O career. And you don't necessarily have to be a great actor. I make a distinction between voice acting and voiceover. Areas like commercials, animation, video games and audiobook narration call for voice acting. Animation, video games and audiobooks in particular require a lot of emotion and characterization. But there's not much call for acting in an announcer tag that reads, "2.9% APR financing for 60 months." That calls for solid articulation, interpretation and resonance, as do many areas of non-voice acting, like instructional or documentary narration; all of which instructors, public speakers and on-air talent possess. I know many people who make a very good living voicing announcer tags and instructional materials.

WHEN COPY STARTS
WITH A QUESTION

A lot of copy and text starts with a question, because the writer wants to pique the listener's interest and draw them into the story with a scenario that may be familiar. Sometimes the question is literally a question—they want to know what you think or wonder if you've ever had a problem that could be solved by their product or service. Other times the question is rhetorical, and in that case, you and they already know the answer to the question.

If it's an actual question, ask the question sincerely. Here's how to do this in a believable way: 1) ask the person you're talking to if you can ask them a question, or 2) tell them you're going to ask them a question.

So, before the copy starts, set it up with either of two prompts: "Let me ask you a question" or "Can I ask you a question?" Then take a beat and then ask the question that starts the copy.

If you put yourself in "question mode" before asking a question, the question you ask will sound more sincere, conversational and believable.

WHEN THERE'S NO NEED
TO READ

M ost voice actors have been taught to keep their eyes on the page when they're reading. Taking your eyes off the page (and the words) is supposed to be a sure-fire way to bollix up your narration. Well, there's some truth to that, but it depends on what you're narrating.

If you're narrating long-form text, taking your eyes off the page is a no-no. E-Learning modules, non-fiction audiobooks, training manuals—these dense forms of text require you not only to keep your eyes glued to the page, they require you to have chameleon-like eyes that scan the page as you're reading.

But, there are many times you don't need to have your eyes on the page. The first place to apply that is a tag line. Look at the copy below:

V-O: The people who tell you to change your oil every 3000 miles...change oil for a living. The people who tell you to change your oil every 5000 miles? They sell cars for a living. And the people you can trust to give you the right oil change schedule based on how, what and where *you* drive? They work *here* for a living. At Oil Depot. Where our trained experts and exclusive Oil Analyzer will give you the one number...that's right for you. Drop by the Depot. Oil Depot.

Look at the tag line: "Drop by the Depot. Oil Depot." After you've rehearsed it a few times, is there any reason to have your eyes on the page when you get to that tag line? No! *There's no need to read that line.* So you can lift your eyes off the page and deliver that line believably and not sound like you're reading it.

Stage actors do this all the time. When they're rehearsing a play and attempting to memorize their lines (called "getting off-book"), they hold the script in one hand and glance at their lines while rehearsing. If they're doing a dialogue, they'll glance at their line and then look at the other actor they're talking to and *speak their line,* not read it. It's called "lifting" lines, and it's a great way to sound authentic and not read *because you're not reading.*

What other times can we not read? When we're asked to do a wild line or pick-up line. If it's short, and we're asked to give the director "three in a row" (sometimes called a "series of three," where you're asked to give the director three slightly varies reads in a row)), again, there's no need to read. Anthem-type spots are other great places to lift your lines. Look at the spot below:

V-O: For all the things you care about.
 For safer roads, skies and buildings where you work and play.
 For cleaner air and water. Safer food and toys.
 Fewer emissions and more energy sources.
 For everything in the world that's important to you, and will be to your children.
 For people. For the planet.
 American Equipment Company. For the better.

These are very short lines, easily lift-able. You look at them, then get your eyes off the page, and speak the lines. They sound authentic and sincere and heartfelt because you're speaking the words instead of reading them.

Another genre where you can sometimes get away with not reading is in interactive videogames. Many times you're asked to deliver short lines spoken by your character, and you're asked (as you are many times) to give the director a series of three. Once you've read the line, unless you have really bad short-term memory, you can usually remember the line without having your eyes on the page.

Apply this technique as much as you can. The more you do it the easier it gets. Just remember that there are many opportunities to not read when you don't need to.

WHO ARE YOU TALKING TO?

One subject all voice acting instructors agree on is that in order to sound believable, you need to sound like you're talking to the listener. And in order to do that, the actor has to pretend like he or she is talking to someone. But you're not always talking to just one person. To who or whom you're talking depends on the copy. Figure out who you're talking to in the following copy excerpts:

V-O: I remember the exact moment I decided to go to Pier 1. I was right here in the kitchen, setting the table, when I noticed that my big centerpiece was a roll of floral-print paper towels. I mean, how sad is that? So I went to Pier 1 and got this great, kind of leafy, fall candle holder and a matching table runner. Now never again will I be the woman with the paper towel centerpiece.

This woman sounds like she's talking to a friend—one person—either on the phone or right there in the kitchen. How about this one:

WAITER: And what can I get for you all this evening? We've got two Macaroni Grill Specials: Chicken that's hand-breaded with Parmesan cheese, herbs and garlic. Or our pasta Alfredo made with four (4) Italian cheeses.

It's obvious from the copy that our waiter's talking to a table of more than one. Okay, who are you talking to in this one?

SFX: car burning rubber

V-O: <u>That's</u> the actual sound of BF Goodrich G-Force Tires setting another new record for street tire performance. And <u>this</u> is the sound...

SFX: crowd cheering

V-O: ...of happy customers, who just found out that if you buy a set of the world's hottest street tires, you get $50 off an alignment that'll help your tires last longer, and your vehicle track straight as a laser.

Easy one, eh? You're most likely talking into a microphone or a camera while at a racetrack, broadcasting either on radio or TV. How about this one? Who are you talking to?

V-O: Today she ran into your room at 4 a.m. to tell you she thinks a leprechaun lives next door. At 7 she decided your heels are a great place to hold dog food. And by 9 you've done the chicken dance ten times. Most people's days have just begun, but you're right in the middle of yours. And you wouldn't trade it for the world. Because at 11 she'll sing that song you taught her, while you quietly brush her hair. And at 3 you'll make her laugh so hard she snorts when you show her how to make a blade of grass sound like a duck. And when you tuck her in for bed, and she reaches for her goodnight hug, you'll ask yourself, "How did we create something so amazing?"

Hopefully, you guessed...yourself. Yes, you're reminiscing, musing over the day's events; past, present and future.

Just remember that you're not always talking to one person. Look at copy carefully to understand the story and discern who you're talking to.

PHONE-PATCH/ISDN
SESSION TIPS

A lot of spots used to be directed live, with a director in the studio with the talent and engineer. Nowadays, a lot of sessions are directed via phone-patch, ISDN, Source Connect or Skype. Sometimes these sessions are a breeze, but sometimes they can be stress-inducing, so you need to prepare yourself, physically and emotionally.

Phone-patch sessions are conducted using an analog platform: linked phones, so the director is directing the talent over the phone, sight unseen. In a phone-patch session, the studio connection is done over standard phone wires, where the client(s) are listening to everything over the phone and approving all takes, and then the sound files are subsequently uploaded in .mp3 or .wav format to an ftp site or Dropbox for download by the client.

ISDN, a digital platform satellite technology. An ISDN patch connects two or more studios, where all takes are digitally transmitted from one to the other—in real time. The client(s) who are in a studio listen to and approve all takes over big studio speakers, and can hear each take much more clearly than over a phone line—it's as if you were in the next room. They're also paying between $200-$500/ hr. for the privilege. The studio receiving the tracks then finishes the spot(s) in post-production. Source Connect and Skype are currently platforms that are being used increasingly, as they're more affordable than ISDN and deliver better audio quality than phone-patch.

In a phone-patch session, the *fish bowl effect* is magnified, because in addition to the director's comments and directions in between takes, there can be numerous clients listening in and commenting on your performance. Sometimes the director is in the studio with you in a typical phone-patch session, sometimes not. Sometimes the creative director, copywriter, account director, and account executive on the agency side are patched in; on the client side, it's possibly the president of the company, and/or the advertising director. Sometimes the agency people are in the control room with the director and the agency's client is patched-in from another city to sign off on the final takes. Add a few more "chefs" to the mix and you have potentially ten people scrutinizing your every word, syllable, punctuation mark, inflection and breath, all of whom you'll hear through your headphones, except when you're performing a take. You might even book one of these sessions where you're performing a dialogue or multi-part script with actors in other studios in different cities, and the multiple interacting talents will be patched together. Here are some tips to survive the experience and come out smelling like a rose:

- Arrive early, rehearse, mark and time your copy.
- Make sure you de-stress and stretch before entering the booth. Prepare to do multiple takes, changes in direction, pick-ups, wild lines and series of three.
- Keep water on hand, and possibly a green apple (for mouth noise).
- Acknowledge and greet everyone in attendance; if you can, write everyone's name in a corner of your script.
- If you hear conflicting direction from the clients, ask the director for clarification.
- Make sure all notes, changes and deletions are done in pencil.

- Listen, stay focused and consistent—i.e., professional.
- Thank everyone involved—quickly—when the session wraps.
- Remember to take care of talent payment paperwork (if there is any) when you're finished.

VOICE MAINTENANCE
DOs AND DON'Ts

*W*hen you're in the booth:

- *Water, water, water.* Plain water or with a bit of lemon, grapefruit juice or any clear juice with no pulp, cuts down on mucus and clears your mouth and throat a bit.

- Some people swear by *green apples*, Granny Smith or Pippin. They're supposedly extremely helpful in eliminating mouth noise and lip smacks.

-*Throat-Coat Tea* is supposedly another great trick for mouth detritus. It's available almost everywhere.

- If you need to clear your throat, do it gently. If you cough hard you'll hurt your vocal cords. Hum gradually into a cough—the humming often breaks up phlegm. Also, if you have anything like laryngitis, and it persists, see an ENT (Ear, Nose and Throat specialist) immediately. If not, just rest your voice, gargle with warm salt water hourly and get lots of sleep.

DO:

- *Bring water or juice* with you into the booth. Make sure you keep it at arm's length but nowhere near any recording equipment.

- *Use sugar-free throat lozenges* to keep your mouth moist. Ricola Pearls and Grether's Red or Black Currant Pastilles are supposedly the best.

- *Keep your sinuses clear.* A decongestant tablet or allergy spray will work for a short time but possibly dry out your mouth; a saline spray will help a bit, depending on the level of your stuffiness; and a saline rinse can sometimes be helpful. If you find yourself constantly stuffed up, consider consulting an Ear, Nose & Throat (ENT) specialist. If you're diagnosed with a deviated septum you might consider surgery (septoplasty). It will clear your nasal passages (and possibly sinuses) immensely and give you more resonance.

- *Remember to breathe* from your diaphragm and keep your mouth open.
- *Try to incorporate cardiovascular activities* into your schedule. The bigger your lung capacity, the more breath you'll have and the better you'll be able to control your breathing.

- *Warm up before performing.* It's like stretching before a run.

DON'T:

- *Eat a heavy meal* before a session. Rinse your mouth beforehand.

- *Drink coffee, caffeinated tea, soft drinks, milk or dairy products or alcohol* before a session. Caffeine constricts the sinuses and throat and coffee is a diuretic. Soft drinks contain sugar, which dries out your mouth, and milk causes mucus to form and sinuses to congest. As far as alcohol is concerned, it really dries out your mouth and impairs your ability to perform, on many levels.

- *Smoke* before a session. There are myriad problems caused by smoking, the least of which smells up the control room, studio, booth and client.

-*Show up at an audition or session with a cold.* Be respectful of fellow actors. If you get *laryngitis,* don't talk—your vocal cords are inflamed and need to heal. Get lots of sleep and eat lots of *ginger* (like the kind that accompanies sushi). Hot herbal tea with honey and lemon juice helps soothe your throat. If you feel a cold coming on, be careful about using Zicam—zinc in a nasal gel formula; too much zinc can destroy your taste buds. Check out or ask your doctor about Alpha CF, a homeopathic formula, or citrus seed extract in tablet form.

- If you really think your condition will seriously affect your performance, bow out, or talk to the producer so he/she can hear and judge your vocal condition.

- *Ignore a medical condition.* Any persistent cough, shortness of breath, sore throat, dizziness, or anything that can affect your performance should be professionally diagnosed—quickly. Don't procrastinate—conditions usually get worse, not better.

WHY SHOULD YOU CONSIDER A VOICEOVER COACH?

I've been teaching and coaching voiceover for fourteen years now, (and directing and producing V-O talent for thirty-five) and have had the opportunity to work with hundreds of voice actors at all different levels.

A lot of actors love the classroom/studio setting. They enjoy the camaraderie of the class, listening to others perform the same copy, getting ideas from their colleagues. They like the studio setting, and are energized by working with a real director and engineer in a professional V-O studio with a voiceover booth.

But there are a growing number of voice actors who, after studying with me in classes (or who've taken classes with other instructors), subsequently engage me in one-on-one coaching. And most of them have told me that they've made much more progress in the one-on-one format.

Why? Well, a lot of actors have unconventional schedules— some work full- or part-time jobs, some are on the road a lot, and many can't commit to four, six or eight consecutive weeks of classes. Some people need more than a few takes to perfect a read (and you don't have a lot of time in a class setting to do a lot of takes, given that there are at least eight people and only three hours of class time). Others get nervous performing in front of a group (albeit a small one), and find the class "audience" a bit intimidating.

I'm finding that a lot of voice actors are more comfortable working one-on-one with a coach, without an audience or anyone else involved except the coach, concentrating on their strengths and weaknesses, using various exercises until they perfect their V-O skills. They find coaching more individualized and custom-tailored to their skills.

Recently, someone wrote me after seeing a promotional piece I sent out, asking, "Really? Do voice actors really need a coach? I thought after you get training, the rest of your skills are developed in the real world through experience."

It reminded me of an article I read in The New Yorker a couple of years ago (*Personal Best* by Atul Gawande, The New Yorker, October 3, 2011). In it, the author differentiates between teaching and coaching, saying coaching "...is different. (In teaching)... there's a presumption that, after a certain point, the student no longer needs instruction. You graduate. You're done. You can go the rest of the way yourself...This is how elite musicians are taught. Many teachers see their role as preparing students to make their way without them."

But many top-tier, veteran voice talent enlist the services of a coach as much as people who are just starting out. What's the difference? "The concept of coaching is slippery," Gawande says. "Many coaches are not teachers, but they teach. They're not your boss...but they can be bossy. They don't even have to be good at what they're coaching. Mainly, they observe, they judge, they guide."

Athletes have coaches, singers have coaches, and some top musicians have coaches. Yitzhak Perlman is among them, as is

Renee Fleming, the renowned operatic soprano. She refers to coaches as "our outside ears." Fleming says, "I've always enjoyed the luxury of having a set of 'outside ears.'" In my case, as a producer, they belong to the engineer I'm working with, and occasionally my client (the advertiser). Having an extra set of ears to be objective about a performance can be invaluable, not just to me, but also to the talent.

When it comes to coaching (and teaching), I've always concentrated on the eight fundamental skills every professional voice actor needs to bring to every performance: Breathing, Timing, Eye-Brain-Mouth Coordination, Articulation, Consistency, Analysis and Interpretation, Acting and Listening/Taking Direction. It was therefore interesting to read in Gawande's article, that "Good coaches know how to break down performance into its individual components. In sports, coaches focus on mechanics, conditioning and strategy, and have ways to break each of those down, in turn." In voiceover, I also focus on mechanics, conditioning and strategy, and break each of those down as well.

The author explains, "Elite performers, researchers say, must engage in 'deliberate practice'—sustained, mindful efforts to develop the full range of abilities that success requires. You have to work at what you're not good at. In theory, people can do this themselves. But most people do not know where to start or how to proceed."

And that's where coaches can be really helpful. "The coach provides the outside eyes and ears," the author says, "...and makes you aware of where you're falling short."

My job as a teacher/coach is to find and point out a voice actor's strengths and reinforce them, and determine their weaknesses or bad habits so we can mitigate or eliminate them. My other job is to give actors the tools they need to for the rest of their career, so they can consistently improve their performances, including the all-important one of self-direction. I can't be with them physically in the booth, but hopefully I can be there mentally.

Personal Best points out that "...coaching done well may be the most effective intervention designed for human performance. Yet the allegiance of coaches is to the people they work with; their success depends on it. And the existence of a coach requires an acknowledgment that even expert practitioners have significant room for improvement."

So if you've tried voice acting classes or seminars or workshops and feel that you'd like to try a different approach to V-O training, you might consider coaching. A lot of people I've worked with have benefited greatly, telling me that they learned more in one hour of coaching than they had from six weeks of classes (except for the ones who've taken *my* classes!). And now that there are so many V-O forums and V-O groups on Facebook, LinkedIn or related sites, you can ask your colleagues who they've worked with and who they recommend. Hopefully you'll find a great V-O coach who can teach you new things and brings out the best in you.

WHAT A DIRECTOR LOOKS
FOR IN A VOICE ACTOR

Almost every director has a core stable of actors who "get it." These are highly talented people who can hit the ball out of the park on the first pitch, and make reading very challenging copy sound easy. It's their job to make the producer look good to the client—that's one of the reasons why they were brought into the studio in the first place. Directors look for key indicators in an actor that will tell them whether that actor can perform flawlessly in a session. The actor who has all of these abilities will be working a lot. The traits that make for an in-demand V-O actor are:

1) **Consistency.** Great V-O actors are consistent from take to take; in timing, pacing, inflection, breath control, volume, projection, accent and acting. They're able to match their voice for pick-ups and punch-ins. They have consistent energy, not only from take to take, but from the beginning through the end of the spot.

2) **Taking direction.** Top-notch voice actors listen carefully to what the director and/or the client are saying. They pay attention to the director and/or engineer's cues for pick-ups and punch-ins. They scrutinize punctuation, changing it, if necessary.

They also avoid stepping on another actor's lines, unless directed to do so.

3) **Professional behavior.** From the moment a professional voice actor enters the studio door to the moment they exit, they comport themselves as professionals. They shower, shave and dress appropriately, with no noisy clothing or jewelry, no heavy perfume or after-shave lotion. They introduce themselves and try to remember names. They always keep an upbeat, positive attitude. And they keep their questions and/or suggestions pertinent.

4) **Readiness.** Professional voice actors show up early, are warmed up, relaxed and focused. They've taken the time to analyze the script, rehearse, time and mark the copy. They're physically, mentally and emotionally prepared to give everyone involved a stellar performance in a sometimes stressful and compressed amount of time.

5) **Talent.** Standout voice talent put their unique spin on copy. They're believable, they become the character, and they sound like they're talking to the listener, not reading. They're sincere and conversational (when called for). They exhibit versatility and range and they're excellent at ad-libbing. In other words, they not only bring the copy to life, but they infuse it with energy and appropriate interpretation.

WHY YOUR FIRST TWO TAKES
ARE SO IMPORTANT

O kay, you won the audition and now it's time for the session. You get yourself situated in the booth, the engineer has gotten a level, and you've been introduced to the client(s) (remotely—it's a phone-patch session). You take a deep breath, part your lips and begin Take 1.

This take speaks volumes, so to speak. Here's why:

1) It immediately tells the director if you're prepared. He or she is listening to hear if you've reprised your audition. I call it "audition love"—they loved your audition—that's why they picked you. Your job is to repeat what they fell in love with. That's the advantage you have going into the session: you're a known quantity, and they're on your side. They just want you to do what you did in the audition! Sure, they may tweak it a bit, but basically, you just have to remember what you did in the audition. And that's so easy! All you have to do is burn your audition to a CD (or a flash drive) and play it in the car on the way to the audition (if you're going to a commercial studio). You'll listen to it numerous times and talk along with it, so you remember the pitch, cadence, intonation, projection and anything else you put into your audition performance.

If the session is one where you didn't audition previously, then the first take tells the director if you understand the tone and concept of the script.

2) It tells the director how confident you are. People can hear confidence a mile away, and it affects your performance. But if you're just starting out, a little bit of nervousness is common.

3) It gives the director a good idea of whether it's going to be a short session or a really long one. If you're having problems navigating through the script on your first take—if you're dropping words, having problems with articulation, pacing and breath control—any hope the director has of getting through the session quickly are dashed.

The solution? Be a Boy or a Girl Scout: just be prepared!

Your second take tells the director many things about you:

1) Did you hear their direction—and take it? A good director will ask you to make adjustments in the copy or your delivery after the first take. The second take tells them if you applied those directions and incorporated them into the copy.

2) Are you consistent? If the second takes is wildly different from the first one, the director will hear you as inconsistent. If that's the case, it'll be difficult for him or her to edit different parts of different takes together (if they have to). There's a saying, "Consistency is the hobgoblin of small minds," but consistency in voice acting (particularly commercials) is really important. An inconsistent voice actor will make the director tear what little hair they have left out of their head.

3) Is this going to be a short or long session? If you're making a number of mistakes or having a difficult time navigating through the copy, that'll indicate to the director that it'll be a long session. Get through it effortlessly and they'll be happy, knowing the session will be short and sweet.

THE V-O REPORT CARD

I devised my V-O Report Card after 35 years of directing voice talent, working with hundreds of voice actors around the world, in scores of studios. And after working with these actors it became apparent that they had developed, like all pros do, "chops." You know what chops are, right? Chops are skills; it's proficiency—the proficiency of professional storytelling. Now, you don't have to be a great actor to tell a story. But, if you want to be a professional storyteller, you need to know how to tell a story well—how to make it compelling.

My V-O Report Card was inspired by what I do on a daily basis: write, cast and direct voice talent for Radio and TV commercials, narrations and many other projects. And I've identified *eight major skills* that every professional voice talent incorporates into each performance. The voice actors who work consistently—and it goes without saying, garner repeat business—score high in every category.

When I teach voice acting—whether in workshops, seminars, webinars, classes in-studio or one–on–one sessions via phone or Skype—I apply the same standards to my students as I do with the talent I hire to perform in my commercials. That way I know that I'm giving them the tools they need to compete in the real world.

When you've been cast to be the talent in a recording session, the director is unconsciously grading you in these eight categories: **Breathing, Timing, Eye-Brain-Mouth Coordination, Articulation, Analysis & Interpretation, Consistency, Acting,** and **Listening to and Taking Direction.** Talk about multi-tasking!

Those actors who score high in each of these categories are working (or will be working) a lot. And chances are they've attained the results of the "10,000 Hour Rule." For those not familiar with this concept, it's the idea that after 10,000 hours of practice at a certain craft or skill, one becomes competent. My sense, though, is that after 20,000 hours one becomes proficient. I've defined each of these categories and broken them down into their various sub-categories. But when you break down these major skills into more nuanced ones, multi-tasking is an understatement!

Look at the first skill: **Breathing**: Breath control is everything; the phrasing's all on the breath. But it's so much more than that; it's control of your pitch, your intonation, your volume, your projection, your inflection, your texture, placement, intensity and energy.

Next, there's **Timing**: Reading to time; 10s, 15s, 30s, 60s and every variation thereof—sometimes even within a tenth of a second—by yourself or in a group; but there's also cadence and pacing, and a mastery of comic or dramatic timing in a monologue or dialogue.

Next is a skill I call **E-B-M**, or **Eye-Brain-Mouth Coordination**. This skill is the marriage of mental and muscle memory of your lips, tongue and teeth where text goes in through your eyes, around your brain and out of your mouth: It's being able to read the script without omitting, adding or changing words/phrases; without stumbling or hesitating; It's being cognizant of the details: honoring punctuation and text treatments like italics, bold, underlines and caps. It manifests itself clearly in your cold reading ability, letting you lift words off the page effortlessly.

Articulation, pronunciation, enunciation, whatever you want to call it—this is a given. Articulating words and phrases clearly and cleanly; no over-articulation, nor under; no sibilance, swallowing, dropping off, fading or popping your plosives for a palpably perilous performance. Always making sure we're in the Goldilocks area of pronunciation: Not too much and not too little, unless it's a character.

Analysis and interpretation is the ability to dissect the script; discern your target audience; and apply the appropriate delivery. It's being able to understand that context determines the right emphasis, in order to make sense of your sentences; and it's also the ability to understand not just the text, but also the subtext. Easy as pie, right? It also involves interpreting the stupid, confusing, nonsensical, and unintentionally hysterical directions you sometimes get along with your script.

Consistency not only means being consistent from take to take, timing-wise and character-wise; you also have to be consistently excellent in every other category listed here!

Acting. I make a distinction between voiceover and voice acting. I relegate voiceover into non-acting roles: legal disclaimers, e-Learning courses, any kind of instructional material, and non-fiction audiobooks—that kind of stuff. Voice acting covers characterization; it's emoting convincingly. It's all about establishing and maintaining the appropriate tone and attitude. However, the thing that both voiceover and voice acting share—always—is the ability to tell a story compellingly by sounding authentic and conversational.

There's a lot of **listening** going on in a session. They're listening to you while you're listening to yourself—remembering what you did; listening to the director—and incorporating their feedback into your subsequent take by making adjustments, listening to your partner or partners if you have them. And you can take that one step further, because the best voice actors listen to other voice actors they admire—for inspiration and motivation.

Wow. Seems a bit overwhelming. And taken all at once, it is, a bit. But you can break it down. You can practice to make your performances better and better and better—and occasionally you'll get one that comes out just perfectly.

Every student in my courses gets my V-O Report Card at the end. It's like an X-ray of their skill-sets. I grade on a 1-10 scale to show areas where they're strong and areas they need to work on. It may show that they're achieving 9s and 10s on all fronts, technically and artistically, or it may show lower numbers—initially. But I have a disclaimer at the end: *"The information contained here constitutes a basic assessment of your present voice-over acting skills and does not reflect other areas of professionalism such as preparation, practice and rehearsal skills, attitude, marketing skills, learning curve, dedication to the craft and other factors outside the purview of class."*

How do you score in *these* areas?

Preparation. This needs to be done physically and artistically.

Stretching. Do you warm up before every audition and session? Or do you think, "I'm okay. I don't really need to stretch." But you do!

Singing. Gently stretching your vocal cords, mouth, lips and face as well as your body before an audition or session will give you more stamina, more flexibility and more control.

Rehearsing. Have you rehearsed, marked and timed your copy, or do you just say, "Ah, I'll just wing it. I do much better at spontaneous cold reads." I have two letters for that: B.S. The more familiar you are with the copy, the easier you'll be able to navigate through it and the less you'll need to rely on the words.

Practicing. Practice always makes better, and sometimes makes perfect. Reading out loud every day strengthens your Eye-Brain-Mouth coordination—i.e., your cold reading skills. It's also the only way to hone your chops.

Attitude. Having a positive, proactive attitude is a must in this business. As an actor, you've got to show that side to all your clients. And that attitude also applies to your marketing skills, because this is, after all, show business. Yeah, it may be an anonymous side of the business of show, but it's still a business and you have to be in self-promotion mode 18/7.

Learning Curve. What kind of training are you involved in to help you achieve professionalism in voiceover? Classes, seminars or workshops? One-on-one coaching? Reading articles, listening to, watching or participating in webinars? Watching YouTube instructional videos? Attending V-O conventions? All of the above? There's never been a more opportune time to get all the knowledge you need from super-qualified instructors who know the lay of the V-O land and can help you navigate it.

Dedication To The Craft. What are you doing to further your V-O performance and career? Participating in V-O work-out groups? Attending meet-ups to network? Joining voiceover groups on Facebook, LinkedIn, V-O Universe, and VoiceoverXtra? Watching top voice talent and coaches online or on VO Buzz Weekly and more? Trying to learn something new every day about voiceover? Contributing and sharing info with the voice acting community? Going those extra steps can pay off in big ways. What's amazing is that there's so much great information available on what it takes to be successful in voiceover, and it's so easy to get.

These are areas of voiceover I can't teach, but hopefully can instill and inspire. Like the eight categories in my V-O Report Card, these are skills you acquire and strengthen when voice acting is something that you eat, sleep, breathe and dream.

A 21ˢᵀ CENTURY RANT

I want to take this opportunity to ask all voice actors everywhere to set your clients—and yourselves—straight on the
pronunciation of the current year, in this second decade of the
21ˢᵗ century.

This book was published in 2014, which I pronounce (along
with many of my colleagues) "twenty-fourteen"—not "two thousand fourteen." At present, about 50% of voice actors use the
former pronunciation, and the other half, the latter. Why the
discrepancy?

When our planet celebrated the millennium, it was exciting!
The year 2000! How futuristic-sounding! Baby boomers thought
we'd have flying cars by then and colonies on the moon. It was cool
to even utter the words "two thousand." An entire generation had
grown up seeing—and saying—"2001—A Space Odyssey" forty years
before. So when 2000 arrived, followed by 2001, we were hooked on
putting "two thousand" in front of all the years afterward.

But keep this in mind: a century ago, when the world ushered
in the 20ᵗʰ century—the year 1900—we didn't call it "one thousand
nine hundred." We called it "nineteen hundred." The same thing
for the previous century, and the ones before that.

The following year we said "nineteen oh one" and so on. And when we got to the first year of the second decade of the 20th century, we said "nineteen ten."

So here's my argument: For the first ten years of the 21st century, considering our romance with the words "two thousand," I think we needed to change our pronunciation once we got to 2010. At that point, the pronunciation should have been "twenty-ten, twenty-eleven, twenty-twelve," etc. Many folks started doing just that, but there have been way too many stragglers.

So voice actors, pick up the 21st century banner and inform your clients that saying "twenty" instead of "two thousand" is hipper, cooler—and saves us from saying one more syllable. And I guarantee you this: by the time the year 2020 comes along, *everyone* will be saying "twenty-twenty."

GLOSSARY OF VOICEOVER TERMS

T his glossary of terms used in the field of voiceover, or voice acting, is one of the most comprehensive compilations of terms
available. It's been distilled from many sources (see bibliography)
and is fairly up-to-date. A few words and phrases may be arcane,
but I wanted to be as inclusive as possible. If you find some of my
definitions lacking in scope and/or specificity, or if you feel that I've
left out some terms, I encourage you to send me your suggestions or
suggested revisions, and if they help clarify the definition I'll incorporate it into any revised editions of this book.

AFTRA: American Federation of Television and Radio Artists, the
old union for Radio and TV actors and voice actors. In 2008 it offi-
cially joined with SAG, the Screen Actors Guild, to form SAG/AFTRA.

account: An advertiser, also referred to as a client.

Account Executive: The person at an ad agency who serves as
a liaison between the agency and the client.

ADR: Automated Dialogue Replacement in a film. A process
where actors replace dialogue in a film or video.

ad lib: A spontaneous spoken addition or alteration to a written script.

agent: A licensed person working at a talent agency who represents talent and either calls them into their facility to audition, sends them scripts to audition in their home studio (and send in via email) or arranges for an actor to audition for casting directors and producers. They also negotiate talent fees and handle talent payments.

air: Also known as *airtime,* it's the media time slotted for a commercial, hence the term *on the air.*

air check: A recorded portion of a radio program for demonstration purposes. Sometimes advertisers ask for air checks to prove if a particular commercial ran at a specified time.

ambience: The continuous background sound behind voice-over placing the monologue or dialogue in a specific setting, like a hospital, restaurant, retail store, gas station, outdoors, etc. In films, the background noise (people talking, in particular) is referred to as *walla.*

analog: The old way of processing and recording sound on tape. Analog recording is still alive and well, but most people today are used to hearing digital recordings, currently in .mp3 format.

animatic: A rough, animated version of a TV spot, usually with storyboard images set to music and voice-over, for a client presentation of a concept.

announcement: A commercial or non-commercial message. Also referred to as a *spot,* it's usually delivered by a spokesperson.

announcer: The role assigned to a voice-actor that usually has non-character copy. Abbreviated as ANN, ANNC or ANNCR on scripts.

articulation: Clear enunciation or pronunciation.

attitude: How a spokesperson or character feels about a certain product or service, or how an actor comes across in general.

audio: Transmission, reception or reproduction of sound.

audition: A free, speculative performance where voice talents read copy in a proposed script. It could take place at an agent's office, a talent's home studio, a casting director's office, or a production company's studio. Usually the best actor is selected for the final job... usually.

availability: The time and date an actor is available for a session. Advertisers or producers will call an agent or manager to find out about an actor's *availability* for a particular job.

back bed: The instrumental end of a jingle, usually reserved for location, phone numbers, legal disclaimers, or any other information the advertiser needs to add.

background: What's placed behind the voice-over track, usually a music bed, jingle or sound effects.

balls: A deep, resonant sound. A crude reference to an actor's testicles, implying that the bigger they are, the deeper their voice is.

bed: The music under an announcer's voice. In a typical 30-second jingle, the bed is usually about twenty seconds long, leaving five seconds for the sing at the beginning and end of the spot.

billboard: The rectangle, or "billboard" drawn around the client name and/or product on a voice actor's script (with a pencil), where emphasis is given to introduce the product. It's a form of marking copy to remind the talent to not throw away the name of the company that's paying them.

bleed: Noise from the headphones being picked up by the microphone or from other ambient sources, like other tracks or performers. Or it can be when two microphones are too close to each other—or not separated—during recording.

board: The audio control center from which the engineer operates. The audio engineer has hundreds of knobs, faders and buttons that adjust the various elements in a Radio spot or jingle. Also known as a *console*.

booking: A decision and commitment on the advertiser's part to hire you for a session. The client calls the actor or actor's agent to *book* an actor for a job. Your agent would say, "You have a *booking* at 1PM tomorrow."

boom: An overhead mic stand.

booth: An enclosed, sound-dampened or soundproofed room where voice talent work, sometimes with ventilation.

branching: Recording one part of a sentence with variables within that sentence as a means of customizing a response. Often recorded for multimedia games and voice mail systems. Also known as *concatenation*.

breakup: When vocal audio becomes distorted and unstable, usually caused by equipment problems or telephone or electrical line interference.

bump: Either to remove a person from a casting list, or as an additional amount of studio time in a session. Also known as a *bumper*.

butt-cut: When sound files are placed together tightly, particularly for a V-O demo.

button: A single scripted or improvised word, phrase or sentence at the end of a spot that closes a commercial without introducing additional copy points. Also refers to a musical punctuation at the end of a jingle. See *sting*.

buy: As in, "That's a buy." Also known as a *keeper*. It's the take the client selects as the best. *Buy* also refers to the amount of money spent on the media time for a commercial spot or campaign.

buy-out: A one-time fee paid for voice-over services on a commercial. A buy-out supplants residuals. Common in most non-union projects.

cadence: The ebb, flow and pace of narration;

call-back: A second shot at an audition. One step closer to booking the job.

call letters: The letters assigned to a Radio station by the FCC. Stations east of the Mississippi River have call letters starting with W, while stations west of the Mississippi have call letters starting with K.

call time: The time scheduled for an audition.

cans: Another word for headphones.

cattle call: An audition where hundreds of people try out for a part on a first-come, first-served basis.

CD-ROM: Compact Disc-Read Only Memory.

character: The person an actor is cast as in a commercial, or the role performed by an actor in a commercial, an animated series, e-Learning module, videogame, web video or audiobook.

Class A: National network commercial usage. Includes the top three U.S. markets (Los Angeles, Chicago and New York), and usually includes TV spot use.

cold read: An audition where an actor is given no time to rehearse and has to read the copy or text "cold."

color: Speech nuances in intonation that give texture and shading to words to make them interesting and meaningful.

commercial: Also referred to as a *spot*, it is a pre-recorded message which advertises a product or service.

compression: Reduces the dynamic range of an actor's voice. Engineers apply compression to *cut through* background music and sound effects.

conflict: Doing two commercials for the same kind of product. An agent will clarify with the client whether doing a specific spot would put an actor *in conflict*, e.g., a voice talent that's voicing the current campaign for Toyota would be in conflict auditioning for any other carmaker.

console: A large desk-like piece of equipment (also known as the *board*) where the audio engineer monitors, records and mixes a voice-over or music session.

control room: Where the engineer and producer (and many times, the client) are located, behind the console. This is usually a separate room from the *booth*.

copy: Also known as the *script*. It's the text of a spot.

copy points: The specific benefits of a product or service, placed throughout the script by the copywriter.

Creative Director: The person at the ad agency responsible for the work of all the other creatives. They oversee Radio and TV, print, outdoor, Internet, direct mail and point of purchase advertising (in-store graphics).

Cross-talk: When copy spoken into one actor's microphone is picked up by another mic. The sound is said to *spill over* or *bleed* into the other actor's mic.

cue: An electronic or physical signal given to an actor to begin performing.

cue up: Matching to time and speed, lining up an actor's voice to the visuals or music.

cut: A specific segment of the voice-over recording, usually referred to during editing.

cut and paste: The act of assembling different *takes* into a composite, edited whole.

cutting through: When a voice "slices through," or doesn't get drowned out by music and sound effects.

DAT: An abbreviation for digital audiotape, high-quality audiotape used in sound studios.

dead air: When a voice-over pause is too long or the station is temporarily not airing any content for a brief amount of time.

decibel: A unit for measuring the intensity of sound. 0 would be no sound, 130 would cause acute aural pain.

de-esser: A piece of equipment used to remove excess *sibilance,* or hissy s's.

demo: A demonstration of an actor's voice talent, representing the actor when they cannot be present physically. Originally in tape and cassette format, demos (now called V-O demos) are now in CD format or digitally "live" on an actor's website, landing page or talent agency roster. Also, a demo is a format used by ad agencies to present an idea to a client.

Demo rate: An actor is paid a *demo rate* to perform a *demo session.* These *demos* are usually not broadcast, but if they are accepted as is, the *demo* is *upgraded* to the final spot.

demographics: The components that describe the advertiser's *target audience.* This is determined by age, sex, income, education, etc.

dialogue: A script calling for two people (or more) talking to each other.

digital recording: A process where sound is digitally converted into ones and zeroes and stored on a DAT, CD, thumb drive, computer hard drive, external drive or the cloud.

director: The person responsible for giving an actor direction in an audition, session or class.

distortion: Fuzziness or breakup in the sound quality of a recorded piece.

donut: A section of a spot that will usually feature another voice, usually an announcer. Many times it's the section of a jingle that showcases an announcement.

double: A term for a two-person spot, or *dialogue*. Also nice to hear when coupled with the word "scale", where the talent would earn twice the union rate for a commercial.

drive time: The most frequently listened to times on the Radio. *Morning drive* refers to the hours between 6AM and 10AM; *evening drive* refers to the slot between 3PM and 7PM, the typical times for rush hour.

drop off: Not ending strong at the end of a word or phrase, or a sudden decrease in volume in a spot or jingle.

drop out: A minute moment of silence inside a recorded spot.

dry mouth: A condition where your mouth has little or no saliva, causing a lot of mouth noise.

dub: Also called a *dupe* (as in duplicate), it's copy of a spot or spots on cassette, DAT or CD. The verb *to dub*, or *dubbing* is the process of transferring recorded material from one source to another.

dubbing: This dubbing is the process of dialogue replacement in a foreign film, as in *dubbing* a French voice into English.

earphones: Also known as *cans*, *headphones* or *headsets*. Worn during the session to hear your own voice as well as cues and directions from the engineer or producer. Also used to converse with the client during an ISDN or phone-patch session.

echo: A repetition of sound.

editing: The removal, addition or re-arrangement of recorded material. Voice elements can be spread apart, slowed down, speeded up, clipped, eliminated, etc. to achieve the final *take*.

EFX: Effects. Another term for *SFX*.

ellipsis: Three periods in a row that usually signify a pause or a hanging, unfinished thought. Plural: ellipses.

engineer: The person who operates the audio equipment during a voiceover or music session.

equalization: Also known as *EQ*, it is used to determine and assign certain frequencies, which can alter the sound of a voice.

eye-brain-mouth coordination: What every good voice actor has to have. It's that loop/connection where words go in through the eyes, hopefully makes sense in the brain and exit through the mouth. It's the ability to "lift" the words off a page effortlessly, without omitting words, adding them or stumbling through them.

FCC: The Federal Communications Commission. Created in 1944 to regulate all interstate and foreign communications by Radio and TV.

fade: To increase (fade up) or decrease (fade down) the volume of sound.

fade in/fade out: When you turn your head away from the mic or towards it. Or when an engineer manipulates the level of the beginning or ending of a voice or music track.

false start: Situation where a talent makes a mistake within the first line or two of copy. The *take* is stopped, the actor restarts and the take is either deleted or re-slated.

feedback: A distorted, piercingly high-pitched sound, usually emanating from headphones or speakers. Many times caused by problems with the console or headphones getting too close to the microphone.

filter: What engineers use on a voice track to make an actor sound different than they normally sound.

fish-bowl effect: When the actor in the booth cannot hear what the engineer or producer is saying, or vice versa.

fluctuation: How often a voice goes up or down, also known as *inflection*. But there can also be fluctuation in the volume of a voice or sound track, sometimes referred to as *flutter*.

foley: Also known in the business as a Foley Stage, this is a special sound stage used for source sound effects. Foley is used to record up-close sound effects for film or video, where the Foley artists match sound with picture, such as walking, running, doors opening or closing, glass breaking, etc.

franchised: Term applied to talent agents who adopt SAG/AFTRA guidelines.

front bed: The opposite of the back bed, where the announcer copy is at the beginning of a jingle.

gain: The volume of a voice, or a fader on the console, as in "raise the gain."

gig: A job.

gobos: Portable partitions positioned around the actor to absorb sound, or to isolate an actor from another on-mic actor.

good pipes: Description of a talent with vocal strength, authority and resonance.

go up for: To audition or to be considered for a job. "I'm *up for* a Ford national," means that an actor is in contention for a national network commercial for Ford.

hard sell: Approach used for high volume retail clients. One producer refers to hard sell as: "I'll stop shouting when you start buying!" Unfortunately, many advertisers (particularly local ones) still think that the louder they shout, the better you'll hear their message.

harmonizer: Also referred to as a *Munchkiniser*, it's a piece of equipment designed to change the pitch of the voice—usually upward. The current technology is known as *pitch-shifting*.

headset: A set of headphones. See *cans*.

high speed dub: A copy of a tape or CD made at several times normal speed.

highs: The high frequency sound of a voice.

hold: When a potential client likes an audition enough to *hold* some of an actor's time for a possible booking—a step before the booking. Usually the client is deciding between a couple of potential voice talent candidates and wants to cover their bets.

holding fee: The money an actor receives if the client wants to *hold* a spot for airing at a later date.

hook: A strong, memorable, simple (sometimes repetitive) tune, most times the chorus section of a song or jingle.

hot: Term used to describe a mic that's on.

house demo: An agency's voice acting talent, the condensed version (each actor has only a one minute demo) of their roster of male and female talent.

in-house: A production produced for the client in the client's own facilities.

in the can: A phrase connoting that a part of the copy or the entire spot is acceptable and done.

inflection: The raising or lowering of voice pitch—a way of reinforcing the meaning of a word by changing the way it is said. See also *fluctuation*.

ISDN: Integrated Services Digital Network. Special high-quality lines that allow voice recording to be digitally transmitted from one recording facility to another in real time during a recording session.

jingle: A musical commercial, in 30 or 60-second format.

laundry list: A string of copy points—adjectives or prices and items in the copy; sometimes a list of benefits of the product or service. The object for the talent is to read them with slightly different emphases.

lay it down: Another phrase meaning "let's record."

lay out: Don't speak, as in "Lay out while the music plays in this section."

level: To set a voice at the optimal point. When the engineer says, "Let's get a level," the actor will start reading the copy *at the level they'll be speaking throughout the spot.*

library music: Pre-recorded music that producers use when the budget doesn't allow for original music to be written and produced. Each piece of music requires a modest fee to be paid, or licensed, usually on an annual basis, sometimes on a buyout basis.

lines: The copy that's read by the voice talent. To *run lines* is to rehearse a dialogue with another actor.

line reading: When a producer explains to a voice talent how they want a line read—by reading it to the actor the way they hear it in their head.

live mic: The mic is on and can pick up everything said in the *booth*. That means everyone in the *control room* can hear. See *hot*.

live tag: The copy delivered at the end of a spot by a staff announcer at the Radio station.

local: Refers to the union in a particular locale. Usually accompanied by a number, i.e.: SAG/AFTRA Local 47.

looping: The technology of recording background sound effects and noises for TV or film. Done in *post-production* after the show is recorded.

lows: The low frequency of a voice.

major markets: Refers to the "Big Three": New York, Chicago and Los Angeles. These largest markets pay the most in voice-over work when a spot airs in these locales.

marking copy: Placing different marks above, below, around and in between words and/or in the margins of a script. Best done in pencil, because direction or emphasis may change.

master: The original recording that all *dubs* are made from.

mic: A common form of the word *microphone*.

milking: Stretching words out and giving them as much emphasis as possible, as in *"Milk it."* See *taffy-pulling*.

mix: The blending of voice, sound effects, music, etc. The *final* mix usually refers to the finished product.

monitors: The loudspeakers in the control room.

monologue: One-person copy. Also referred to as a *single* or *solo read*.

mouth noise: The *clicks* and *pops* a microphone picks up from a dry mouth.

.mp3: The name of the file extension and also the name of the type of file for MPEG, audio layer 3. Layer 3 is one of three coding schemes (layer 1, layer 2 and layer 3) for the compression of audio signals. Layer 3 uses perceptual audio coding and psychoacoustic compression to remove all superfluous information (more specifically, the redundant and irrelevant parts of a sound signal. The stuff the human ear doesn't hear anyway. The result in real terms is layer 3 shrinks the original sound data from a CD (with a <u>bit rate</u> of 1411.2 kilobits per one second of stereo music) by a factor of 12 (down to 112-128kbps) without sacrificing sound quality.

multiple: Refers to a script with three or more characters in it.

multi-track: A machine capable of recording and replaying several different recorded tracks at the same time.

music bed: The soundtrack that will be placed behind the copy, or mixed in with it.

non-union: A voiceover job that is paid not through the union. A *non-union* shop is one that is not a SAG/AFTRA signatory, nor abides by their rules.

off-camera: A part where an actor supplies only their voice to a TV spot or video presentation.

on mic/off mic: Either speaking or not speaking directly into the microphone. An actor is *on mic* when recording, but can turn his head to speak *off mic*.

outtake: A take that hasn't been approved and accepted. Sometimes a partial or mangled take.

overlapping: When an actor starts his or her line a moment before another actor finishes theirs. Also known as *stepping on lines*.

over scale: Any amount paid over the wage set by SAG/AFTRA.

over-the-top: Direction for an actor to deliver a broad portrayal of a particular character. It sometimes makes the copy sound larger than life, requiring the actor to overact.

pace: The speed at which an actor reads copy.

paper noise: Sound that the mic picks up as you move your pages/script. Computer tablets and laptops have eliminated the need for most paper scripts, but actors still like using the old standbys of paper and pencil.

patch: To make an electrical/digital/satellite connection for recording and/or broadcast. Also referred to as a *phone-patch, land-patch* or *satellite-patch*. A phone-patch connection is an analog setup, linking two phone lines to or from a studio. A land-patch is a fiber-optic cable connection, using Internet-based programs like Source Connect, and a satellite-patch is a connection where two studios are connected via satellite in an ISDN setup.

paymaster: A payroll service that handles talent payments for the producer or agency. They pay the talent, the agent and the union (SAG/AFTRA) if the session was union-sanctioned.

phasing: When sound reflects or bounces off certain surfaces and causes a weird, disjointed effect in the recording.

phonemes: The small units of sound used to make words.

phones: A short word for *headphones*.

pick-up: Re-recording a section of copy at a certain point. 90% of your read may be *in the can*, but there may be a phrase, sentence or paragraph that the director feels could be done a bit better, clearer, faster, slower, etc. The director tells you exactly where they want you to "pick-up" your line(s)—where to start from and where to end. The actor reads a sentence or phrase before the pick-up starting point, *reading into* the pickup line, and then a sentence or phrase past the pickup line. This is done to help the engineer better edit the pick-up, matching phrasing and levels.

pick-up session: An additional session to complete the original. There may be copy or direction changes in a spot before it's finally broadcast. This is usually due to the client changing their mind before they commit the spot to *air*.

pitch: The musical level at which a person speaks.

placement: Where the mic is positioned when an actor is reading.

playback: Listening back to what has just been recorded.

plosive: Any consonant or combination of consonants that causes a *popping* noise on the mic.

plus ten: Refers to the contractual agreement in which the producer agrees to add an additional 10% to the actor's payment for the agent's commission.

popping: When voice sounds are registering too hard into the mic. Usually caused by *plosives*.

pop filter: A foam cover enveloping the mic or a nylon or per-forated metal windscreen in front of the mic. Mitigates *popping*. Also known as a *pop stopper* or *mic condom*.

post-production: Also known as *post*. The work done after the voice talent has finished recording the session. This includes mixing in SFX and music.

pre-life/pre-scene: The previous history an actor invents for his character. Also known as a *prompt* or *back story*.

producer: The person in charge of the voice-over session. Many times the producer is also the *director*.

promo: A promotional commercial spot used by TV and Radio stations specifically to increase audience awareness of upcoming TV programming.

protection: Also known as *insurance,* this is an additional take/s requested by the producer to insure that they have a backup of a take they like. Usually phrased as, "One more for protection."

PSA: Public Service Announcement. Commercials produced to raise awareness of current issues, such as smoking, drug abuse, pollution, child abuse, pregnancy, pet adoption, homelessness, etc. or for charities that help fund research into diseases.

punch: Reading a word or line with more intensity.

punch-in: Sometimes referred to as a *pick-up*, it's the rejoining or continuation of a piece of copy. The engineer will *punch in* (record) a *pick-up* at a certain point in the copy, to help with editing later on.

read: The style of reading an actor presents as a voice talent, or your performance, as in, "That was a good read."

real time: An event that takes as long as it actually takes, as opposed to high-speed.

released: Being dropped from consideration from a voice-over job. It's one of two results from being *on hold* or *on avail*. If your agent says you've been released from availability on a certain spot, you didn't book the job—someone else got it.

residuals: Payments an actor receives every thirteen weeks their spot airs (if it's a Radio spot) or for every time a TV spot airs.

resonance: The full quality of a voice created by vibrations in resonating chambers, such as the mouth and sinus areas.

re-use: What actors are paid when their spot is re-run. It's usually the same amount they received for the first 13-week cycle of use.

reverb: A variation of *echo*. It's an effect added to your voice in *post*.

room tone: The sound a room makes without anyone in it. The sound is always recorded for use in audiobooks for continuity.

rough mix: The step before the *final mix*. This is when the producer and engineer fine-tune *levels* of voice, music and sound effects.

run-through: Rehearsing the copy before recording. Like a dress rehearsal.

SAG: Known for decades as the Screen Actors' Guild, the union for film actors and performers, it's now joined forces with AFTRA (American Federation of TV and Radio Artists) to become one union, SAG/AFTRA.

safety: This is a re-take that the producer or client wants to make sure that if there's something technically wrong with the take they like, they have a back up. "Let's do one more for *safety*," is a common phrase. See *protection*.

S.A.S.E.: Self-addressed stamped envelope. Soon to become extinct.

SFX: Shorthand for sound effects. Also seen as *EFX*.

scale: The minimum, established wages set by SAG/AFTRA for working talent. *Double scale* or *triple scale* refers to these wages doubled or tripled.

scale plus 10: Refers to the extra 10% paid to the actor's agent on a job.

scratch track: An initial audio track that a production company or ad agency may ask an actor to read before the project is finally produced (see *animatic*). This is usually done so the client (or advertiser) can see and/or hear the creative approach on a spot or campaign before the final production. This is usually not a paid gig for the performer, but a potential precursor to the actual, paid session.

series of three: Term used to describe a phrase or line of text or copy to be recorded in a set of three. Each read is usually varied slightly in projection and inflection.

session: The event where a talent performs a script for recording purposes.

session fee: Initial payment for a commercial.

shave: To pare down the time of your read, as in, "Can you shave three seconds off that read?"

sibilance: A drawn out or excessive "S" sound during speech. Some sibilance is joined with a whistle. Most engineers mitigate sibilance with a sound tool called a *de-esser.*

sides: Scripts for Radio & TV commercials, animated series or videogames. On some TV scripts, the action (Video) is in the left column and the copy (Audio) is on the right. Sides/scripts for animation and videogames generally use a screenplay layout.

signatory: Someone (usually a producer or ad agency) who has signed a contract with SAG/AFTRA stating that they will only work on union jobs and promise to pay talent union scale.

signature: The specific quality of a voice that makes it unique. Your signature sound is your voiceprint/style of delivery.

single: Also known as a *monologue,* or one-person copy.

slate: Announcing a name and/or a number before a *take*, usually paired with the title of the spot, the name of the advertiser or possibly a character the actor is playing. The slate helps the director and engineer identify and keep track of the actors and the various V-O tracks they record. Most *slates* are announced by the engineer, but sometimes the actors *slate* their own name.

spec: Volunteering your services and postponing payment until a project sells. The popular definition is "working for nothing now on the promise of getting paid if the project is approved and funded later on."

spokesperson: Also referred to as *spokes*. A voice actor who is hired on a repeat contractual basis to represent a product or company in Radio and TV spots.

spot: A commercial. Originated from the days when all commercials were performed live, in between songs played on the radio. The performers were *"on the spot."*

stair stepping: Having your pitch progressively rise up or down as a means of defining phrases. This technique is especially effective when reading *laundry lists*.

stand: A music stand, where copy is usually placed in the *booth* behind, below or in front of a mic. The stand can be manipulated by the actor so they can set the height, distance and angle that's best for them to read their copy.

station I.D.: A short sound bite where the *call letters* of the station are announced or sung.

steps: Increasing the energy on a long list of adjectives or superlatives.

storyboard: The art director's and copywriter's conception of a TV spot or film, drawn on a large board or rendered on a computer for presentation to a client. The talent (and advertiser) gets to see what the on-camera actors are doing in the spot. See *animatic*.

studio: The facility where all recording or filming for a commercial takes place.

sweeps: The TV and Radio ratings periods when the total viewing or listening audience is estimated, thereby determining advertising rates. These occur in February, May and November every year.

sync: Matching a voice from a previous take. Also refers to aligning tracks to start or end together.

taffy-pulling: Stretching out a word or a phrase.

Taft-Hartley: This labor law that allows an actor to not be required to join the union for their first job. But joining SAG/AFTRA is required if an actor is hired for another union job within 30 days of the last job.

tag: Information placed at the end of a commercial containing a date, time, phone number, website address, legal disclaimer, etc. Sometimes a different announcer reads the tag.

take: The recording of one specific piece of voiceover copy. All takes are numbered consecutively, usually *slated* by the engineer.

talent: A broadcast performer, entertainer or voice actor.

talk-back: Refers to the button connected to the microphone in the engineer's console. It allows the engineer or director to talk to the talent in the soundproofed booth.

tease: The introductory line used to promote and pique interest. *Promos* (commercials for TV programming) are sometimes referred to as *teasers*.

tempo: The speed at which copy is delivered. See *pace*.

tight: Not a lot of time to read—referring to a script that has a lot of words and not much time to say them in, e.g., *"This is a really tight :60."*

time: Literally, the length of a spot. Some Radio spots *time* in at 30 or 60 seconds, most TV spots at 30.

time code: A digital read-out on the engineer's console referring to audiotape or videotape positions. Used in film dubbing, but also audio recordings as well.

tone: A specific sound or attitude.

track: Either to record, or the actual audio piece. *"We're ready to track,"* as opposed to *"Listen to this track."*

trailer: A commercial that promotes a film or video release.

undercutting: Dipping down in a sentence and throwing a portion of it away.

units: The number assigned by SAG/AFTRA to different-sized cities throughout the U.S. Each city varies in their amount of unit value by their population. This directly affects the amount of money an actor receives in residuals.

use fee: An additional fee paid to the performer when their spot is actually aired.

Value-added: Refers to words in a script that give the impression you're getting more than you paid for. *Plus, free, new, improved* and *extra* are examples.

voiceprint: The vocal equivalent of a fingerprint. Everyone's voiceprint is unique.

V-O: Short for *voice-over*. Also seen as *AVO* (announcer voice-over). It's the act of providing a voice to a media project, where the voice is sometimes *mixed* with music and *SFX*. *Voiceover* was the term originally used to describe an announcer's voice on a television spot, referring to the process as "voice over picture." The more accurate term now is voice *acting*, which is the art of using the voice to bring life to written words.

VU meter: A meter on the engineer's console that indicates the level of sound passing through the board.

walla: The sound of many voices talking at once, used as background sounds for different scenes in a movie or commercial. Originally, it was thought that saying the words "walla walla" or "rhubarb and garbage" over and over again in the background would simulate the appropriate ambiance for a busy scene, but today actors doing walla converse in the way they would normally do in that situation.

wet: A voice or sound with *reverb* added to it.

wild line: A single line from a script that is re-read several times in succession until the perfect *read* is achieved. It's considered *wild* because it's read separately from the entire script. Sometimes it's performed as a *series of three*, where the actor reads the line three times in a row without interruption. Each line is read slightly differently, unless otherwise directed.

wild spot: A flat fee for a spot that airs for an indeterminate number of times within a 13-week cycle, not broadcast through a national network of Radio and TV stations. Can be local, regional or national.

windscreen: A pop filter, or *pop stopper*.

woodshed: To rehearse or practice reading copy out loud. From the old days of theater where actors would have to rehearse in a woodshed before going out to perform.

wrap: The end, as in, *"That's a wrap."*

Adapted and compiled from the following sources:

James Alburger, *The Art of Voice-Acting;* Focal Press (1999)

Susan Blu & Molly Ann Mullin, *Word of Mouth*; Revised Edition, Pomegranate Press (1996)

Terri Apple, *Making Money in Voice-Overs;* Lone Eagle Publishing Company (1999)

Alice Whitfield, *Take It From The Top;* Ring-U-Turkey Press (1992)

Sandy Thomas, *So You Want To Be A Voice-Over Star;* In The Clubhouse Publishing (1999)

Terry Berland & Deborah Ouellette, *Breaking Into Commercials;* Plume Publishing (1997)

Chris Douthitt & Tom Wiecks, *Putting Your Mouth Where The Money Is*; Grey Heron Books (1996)

Chuck Jones, *Making Your Voice Heard;* Back Stage Books (1996)

Bernard Graham Shaw, *Voice Overs: A Practical Guide;* Routledge Publishing (2000)

Elaine A. Clark, *There's Money Where Your Mouth Is;* Back Stage Books (2000)

DIRECTION TERMS

T hroughout a session, and at the end of every take, you'll probably receive some sort of direction from the producer, hopefully preceded by the phrase, "Good!" or "Great!" There are countless ways for a director to tell you if you're on track, performance-wise—whether or not you're emphasizing the right words or phrases, your timing is good, your enunciation is clear and your overall tone and energy is appropriate. Some musically-inclined directors might use musical terms to get their point across. Others might use acting terminology, or even sports references. And others will have no idea how to articulate their direction, and either give you confusing direction or sometimes rely on the engineer to interpret for them. If you get confusing or conflicting direction, ask for clarification. The following terms can be heard being bandied about in hundreds of studios across the country every day.

"Accent it.": Emphasize or stress a syllable, word or phrase.

"Add life to it.": Give it some oomph—your reading is flat. One expert advises: *"Give it C.P.R.: Concentration, Punch, Revive it!"*

"Add some smile.": Smile when you're reading. It makes you sound friendly and adds more energy to your read. Many times widening your eyes will literally help you smile.

"Be authoritative.": Make it sound like you know what you're talking about. Be informative.

"Be real.": Adding sincerity to your read. Similar to *"make it conversational."* Be genuine and true-to-life in your delivery.

"Billboard it.": Emphasize a word or phrase, most always done with the name of the product or service (see billboard). It reminds you to introduce the advertiser.

"Bring it up / down.": Increase or decrease the intensity or volume or pitch of your read. This may refer to a specific section of the copy or the overall script.

"Button it.": Ad-lib at the end of a spot.

"Color it.": Give a the text or copy various shades of tonality. Look at a script as a black and white outline of picture that you have to color, shade and texture.

"Don't sell me.": Throw out the "announcer" voice, relax; the read is sounding too hard sell. Don't try to convince the listener.

"Fade in / fade out": Turning your head toward or away from the mic as you are speaking, or actually turning your entire body and walking away. This is done to simulate the "approach" or "exit" of the character in the spot.

Also refers to the beginning or end of an audio section where the volume increases or fades out gradually.

"False start": You begin and make a mistake. You stop; the engineer records it as a *false start* and either records over the first slate or begins a new slate.

"Fix it in the mix.": What is done in post-production, usually after the talent or the client leaves. This involves fixing level changes, editing out mouth noises, tightening time between words or lines, etc.

"Flatten your delivery.": Make your performance more monotone, deadpan.

"Good read.": You're getting closer to what they want, but it's not there yet.

"Hit the copy points.": Emphasize the product/service benefits more.

"In the can.": All recorded takes. The engineer and producer refer to this as having accomplished all the takes they need to put the spot together.

"In the clear.": Delivering your line(s) without *stepping* on other actors' lines.

"In the pocket.": You've given the producer exactly what they want.

"Intimate read.": Close in on the mic more, speak with more breath, and make believe you're talking quietly into someone's ear. Sitting helps.

"Keep it fresh.": Giving the energy of your first take, even though you may be on your twentieth.

"Let's lay one down.": Let's start recording.

"Less sell / more sell.": De-emphasizing/stressing the client name/benefits.

"Let's do a take.": The recording of a piece of copy. Each take starts with #1 and ascends until the director finds the one(s) they like. Also heard: "Let's lay it down" or "Let's lay one down."

"Let's get a level.": The director or engineer is asking you to speak in the volume you're going to use for the session. Take advantage of this time to rehearse the copy one more time. Any shouts or yelling will require you to turn your head slightly away from the mic or taking a step back. If the mic needs to be adjusted, the engineer will come into the booth. Do not touch or move the mic unless instructed to do so.

Live tag: This is a sentence or two that is read at the end of a spot by a live announcer on the Radio station staff, not by you.

Live mike: The mike is on and everyone can hear everything you say—before, after and in-between takes. Be very careful what you say in the booth—you never know who may be listening.

"Make it conversational.": Just like it sounds, make your read more natural. Throw out the "announcer" in your read, and take the "read" out of your delivery. If it sounds like you're reading, you won't be believable. Pretend you're telling a story, talking to one or a few persons. Believe what you're saying.

"Make it flow.": Also heard as: "Smooth it out." Avoid choppy, staccato reads, unless the character calls for it. Breathe through your phrases.

"More / less energy.": Add more or less excitement to your read. Use your body to either pump yourself up or calm yourself down. Check with the engineer (i.e., do a level) to make sure your levels are not too loud or soft.

"Mouth Noise.": The pops and clicks made by your mouth, tongue, teeth, saliva and more. Most mouth noises can be digitally removed, but make sure that you don't have excess mouth noise, because too much is an editing nightmare and will affect your work. Water with lemon or pieces of green apple can help reduce or eliminate most mouth noise.

"One more time for protection.": The director wants you to do exactly what you just did on the previous take. This is similar to, "That was perfect, do it again." This gives the director and engineer more selections to play with, should they need them in post-production.

"Over the top.": Pushing the character into caricature. Appropriate when talking to very young children, humorous commercials or some animated series and videogames.

"Pick it up.": Start at a specific place in the copy where you made a mistake, as in, "Pick it up from the top of paragraph two," or "Let's do a pick-up at the top of the second block."

"Pick up your cue.": Come in faster on a particular line. Anticipate your lines when doing a dialogue.

"Pick up the pace.": Pace is the speed in which you read the copy. Read faster, but keep the same character and attitude.

"Play with it.": Have fun with the copy, change your pace and delivery a bit, try different inflections.

"Popping.": Noise resulting from hard consonants spoken into the mic. *Plosives,* which sound like short bursts from a gun, are most evident in consonants like B, K, P, Q and T.

"Punch-in.": The process of recording your copy at an edit point in real time. In a punch-in, as opposed to a "pick-up," the engineer will play back part of the copy you recorded and expect you to continue reading your copy at a certain point. The director will give you explicit directions as to where in the script you will be "punched in," and you will read along with your pre-recorded track until your punch-in point. From there, you'll continue recording at the same level and tone you originally laid down.

"Punch it / push it.": Give it more energy.

"Read against the text.": Reading a line with an emotion opposite of how it would normally be read.

"Romance it.": Also heard as, "Warm up the copy." Make it more intimate, more romantic. Push air over your words to soften them.

"Run it down.": Read the entire script for level, time and one more rehearsal before you start recording.

"Shave it by...": Take a specific amount of time off your read. Also heard as "shave a hair." If your read times out at 61 seconds, the director might ask you to "shave it by 1.5 seconds."

"Skoche more / less.": A little bit, just a touch more or less. This can refer to volume, emphasis, inflection, timing, etc.

"Split the difference.": Do a take that's "between" the last two you just did. For example, if your first take comes out at :58, and your second take comes out at :60, and the director asks you to "split the difference," adjust your pacing so the third take comes in at: 59. Or, if your first take is monotone-ish and your second one is very "smiley" and the director asks you to "split the difference," adjust your read so that the third take will sound somewhat in between the first two.

"Stay in character.": Your performance is inconsistent. Whatever accent and voice you commit to, you have to consistently maintain that voice from beginning to end, take after take after take.

"Stepping on lines.": Starting your line before another actor finishes theirs. Sometimes the director wants actors to "overlap" lines, or interrupt each other. Others want each line *"in the clear,"* where there is no overlapping or *stepping.*

"Stretch it/tighten it.": Make it longer/shorter.

"Take a beat.": Pause for about a second. You may be asked to do this during a specific part of the script, like in between paragraphs, inside of a sentence, as a reaction moment in a dialogue or in a music bed. A good sense of comic timing is particularly helpful in determining the actual length of the beat.

"Take it from the top.": Recording from the beginning of a script.

"That's a buy/keeper.": The take that everyone loves—at least the director loves. If the client loves it, then it's accepted.

"That was perfect—do it again": An inside joke, but a compliment. Usually the producer wants you to reprise your take "for safety," i.e., to have another great alternate take.

"This is a :15/:30/:60": Refers to the exact length of the spot in seconds, also known as a *read* or *take.*

"Three in a row.": Reading the same word, phrase, sentence or tag three times, with variations, but usually not changing the emphasis. Each read should have a slightly different sound, but all should be read in the same amount of time. The engineer will *slate* three in a row with a, b, c or 1, 2, 3.

"Throw it away.": Don't put any emphasis or stress on a certain word or phrase, or possibly the whole script.

"Too much air.": Noise resulting from soft consonants spoken into the mic. Most evident in consonants like F, G, H and W, and word beginnings and endings like CH, PH, SH & WH.

"Under/ over.": Less or more than the time amount needed. If you were *"under or over"* you need to either shorten or lengthen your pace and *"bring it in"* to the exact time.

"Warm it up a little.": Make your delivery more friendly and personal. Whatever makes you feel warm and fuzzy is the feeling you should inject into your delivery.

Adapted and compiled from the following sources:

James Alburger –*The Art of Voice-Acting;* Focal Press (1999)

Susan Blu & Molly Ann Mullin – *Word of Mouth,* Revised Edition; Pomegranate Press (1996)

Terri Apple, *Making Money in Voice-Overs;* Lone Eagle Publishing Company (1999)

Alice Whitfield, *Take It From The Top;* Ring-U-Turkey Press (1992)

Sandy Thomas, *So You Want To Be A Voice-Over Star;* In The Clubhouse Publishing (1999)

Terry Berland & Deborah Ouellette, *Breaking Into Commercials;* Plume Publishing (1997)

Chris Douthitt/Tom Wiecks, *Putting Your Mouth Where The Money Is,* Grey Heron Books (1996)

Chuck Jones, *Making Your Voice Heard,* Back Stage Books, (1996)

Elaine A. Clark, *There's Money Where Your Mouth Is;* Back Stage Books (2000)

COMMANDMENTS

Yeah, I could've called them suggestions or reminders, but they're really commandments: things you should do (or not do) to bolster your voiceover career. And like the others, these are engraved in stone:

◊ EXERCISE AND PRACTICE COLD READING EVERY DAY.

◊ LISTEN CAREFULLY—TO YOURSELF, TO OTHER ACTORS, TO ON-AIR TALENT AND TO THE DIRECTOR.

◊ NEVER CRITICIZE YOURSELF IN FRONT OF OTHERS.

◊ BRING PASSION TO EVERY VOICE ACTING SESSION.

◊ ALWAYS USE PENCIL TO MARK YOUR COPY.

◊ WARM-UP BEFORE EVERY CLASS, AUDITION OR SESSION.

◊ FIND THE MUSIC IN COPY.

◊ REHEARSE AS MUCH AS POSSIBLE BEFORE RECORDING.

◊ NEVER MAKE A DEMO UNTIL YOU'RE READY.

◊ ARRIVE AT EVERY LIVE AUDITION/SESSION EARLY AND PREPARED.

◊ PRACTICE, PRACTICE, PRACTICE: IT SOMETIMES MAKES PERFECT, BUT ALWAYS MAKES BETTER.

◊ REMEMBER THAT VOICE-OVER IS ALSO A BUSINESS.

◊ WHEN APPROPRIATE, AD-LIB AND RE-WRITE.

◊ SOCIALIZE *AFTER* THE AUDITION.

◊ ALWAYS ACT PROFESSIONALLY.

◊ NEVER TELL PEOPLE HOW GOOD YOU ARE. TELL THEM HOW GOOD *THEY* ARE.

◊ BE AVAILABLE 18/7. A MISSED CALL COULD BE A MISSED JOB.

MEMORABLE, QUOTABLE QUOTES

"There are three things you need to have [to enter the field of voice-over]...a decent speaking voice...an ability to act... and the willingness to spend the time necessary to market and promote your talent to get auditions so that you can get the work." [1]

"The better commercials and voice-over work do not sound like someone doing voice-over work. They sound like your best friend talking to you—comfortable, friendly, and most of all, not "announcer-y."" [1]

"Believability is one of the secrets of success in voice-acting... if you believe it, the listener will."[1]

"Technique must be completely unconscious...any performer focused on the technical aspects of the performance cannot possibly be believable." [1]

"Acquiring a skill, and becoming good at the skill, is called competency. Becoming an expert with the skill is called proficiency. You must first be competent before you can become proficient." [1]

"A good performer never stops learning." [1]

"Don't do a demo until you are ready...study acting, do your exercises, take classes and workshops, read books about voice-over and practice your skills and techniques." [1]

"A voice-over is not just someone reading a commercial—it is a particular person, in a particular situation, talking to another particular person (or persons), about a particular product." [2]

"Voice-over excellence requires acting in the finest sense of the word." [2]

"Commercials call for subtleties layered over a base of sincerity." [2]

"Don't place limits on your learning or you will only limit your range and your career. Other people try to limit you enough anyway—don't do it to yourself." [2]

"Keep it natural—believe who you are, and they will believe it, too." [2]

"The very best acting really isn't acting' at all—it's based on reality and what we do naturally, listening and reacting to other people." [2]

"Never critique your work out loud. That is the director's job. If you receive a compliment, say thank you and then—shut up!"[2]

"Take your career seriously, but not the rejections." [2]

"An attribute required by successful voice talents is a very thick skin."—Larry Belling

"It's all just a matter of selection, not rejection."—Paul Kirby

"Training, plus desire and commitment, will result in success."—Ginny McSwain

"Listen to your inner voice so that you can win with your outer voice."—Jennifer Darling

"The best workshops and classes push the artist to grow and learn how to compete and how to win jobs...you don't just learn 'Voice-Over 101' and then 'have it.'"—Ginny McSwain

"The only limits you'll experience are the ones you place on yourself." [2]

"The only difference between you and several hundred others reading for the same job is your personality." [3]

"Voice-overs are for people with personality, flexible voices and acting skills. They are not, however, for those who are lazy or faint of heart." [3]

"Having a great voice isn't enough. Learning what to do with it is the key to a long and lucrative career." [3]

"Voice quality is important, but not as much as rhythm. It's all about rhythm." [3]

"Worry less about how you are going to say it and more on what you are saying." [3]

"Don't worry about 'awful' reads. Remember how many times you thought (and were told) you were 'wonderful' and still didn't get the job." [3]

"If you're not sure how to read something, ask." [3]

"When you have a passion, you can't be discouraged." [4]

"Always maintain your sense of humor. It will never fail you." [4]

"There is one quality that you must have in order to work in this [the voice-over] business: the ability to take direction." [4]

"This business is about listening as much as it is about speaking." [4]

"If you are true to the emotions of the copy, your delivery will have credibility." [4]

"Just because you didn't get the part doesn't mean you've failed."—Les Perkins

"Never bad-mouth another performer. It's a very small business."—Don Peoples

"If you need training, it is better to approach a director rather than a performer. An ancient Chinese proverb states: 'The puppet does not necessarily know how the strings are pulled.'" [6]

"Always make good use of your down time."—Marc Cashman

"Having a good voice is a gift. Knowing what to do with it is the challenge." [7]

"Your voice is your instrument. It needs to be properly warmed up before it can function at full capacity." [7]

"The microphone should be treated like an ear." [7]

"Tell me, don't sell me." —Penny Abshire

"Your attitude is just as important to your success as is your talent." [5]

"Treat your voice-over career as you would a small business." [5]

"To hit a home run in the voice-over major leagues, you have to use the whole package: body, heart and voice." [7]

"Add your own expertise and craftsmanship to build the copywriter's script into a thing of beauty...The copywriter is the architect of the ad. The talent is the carpenter. The script is the blueprint. The studio engineer provides all the necessary construction materials. The producer is the building supervisor." [8]

"Information has to come through when you're really ready to receive it. You may have several coaches, then one will finally get through. It doesn't mean that all the other coaches were bad. It is generally more likely that you were finally ready to receive and apply the information given."—Patty Kallis[9]

"Skill...can be taught, tenacity cannot. There have been...many studies of elite performers—concert violinists, chess grand masters, professional ice-skaters, mathematicians...and the biggest difference researchers find between them and lesser performers is the amount of deliberate practice they've accumulated. Indeed, the most important talent may be the talent for practice itself... Top performers dislike it just as much as others do. But, more than others, they have the will to keep at it anyway.[10]

1. - James Alburger – *The Art of Voice-Acting;* Focal Press (1999)
2. - Susan Blu & Molly Ann Mullin – *Word of Mouth,* Revised Edition; Pomegranate Press (1996)
3. - Terri Apple, *Making Money in Voice-Overs;* Lone Eagle Publishing Company (1999)

4. - Alice Whitfield, *Take It From The Top;* Ring-U-Turkey Press (1992)

5. - Sandy Thomas, *So You Want To Be A Voice-Over Star;* In The Clubhouse Publishing (1999)

6. - Bernard Graham Shaw, *Voice-Overs, A Practical Guide;* Routledge Publishing (2001)

7. - Elaine A. Clark, *There's Money Where Your Mouth Is;* Backstage Books (2000)

8. - Chris Douthitt & Tom Wiecks, *Putting Your Mouth Where The Money Is;* Grey Heron Books (1998)

9. - Terry Berland & Deborah Ouellette, *Breaking Into Commercials;* Penguin Books (1997)

10. - Atul Gawande, excerpt from *"The Learning Curve",* New Yorker Magazine (2002)

WHAT VOICE-ACTING
IS ALL ABOUT

*T*he following is an excerpt of a foreword by Corey Burton from *Scenes for Actors and Voices by Daws Butler*, edited by Ben Ohmart and Joe Bevilacqua (Bear Manor Media 2003). For those of you not familiar with Daws Butler, he was the voice of Yogi Bear, Huckleberry Hound, Quick Draw McGraw, Elroy Jetson, Cap'n Crunch and a hundred others. Among his many voice acting students (he was a teacher, too!) was June Foray, the voice of Rocky the Squirrel, and Nancy Cartwright, the voice of Bart Simpson. Words or phrases in brackets are mine.

"Voice acting is all about 'getting the words off the page.' Performing the [monologue or] dialogue not simply by reading aloud, but delivering the lines as if those words just naturally occurred to the character; as an expression of that character's own thoughts and feelings at that particular moment in their imaginary lives.

Love the words, but don't fall in love with them (or the sound of your own voice). 'Taste' the words: they are delicacies to enjoy, but try not to let the listener hear you 'savoring' them too often. Becoming too attached to the words *exactly as they appear on the page* will often create a stilted and mechanical performance, trapping the actor in a limited or unnatural range of expression.

It is far more important to express the emotion behind the word, than to actually feel that emotion while you're doing it; and clearly sounding the word is not really necessary for the listener to know it's there: so long as the meaning and emotion behind the word is clearly communicated within the context of the speech.

Voice Acting is very much like Jazz: the words represent the melody, but are open to 'interpolation.' They may be molded, changed or enhanced, as your character would see fit. Nothing is 'written in stone.' So long as the intention, or meaning, is the same, you are not showing any disrespect for the writer by making the words 'your own.'

As with music, the timing and pauses between words and phrases can be just as important as the words themselves. A prime example would be Jack Benny, of whom it was said that his greatest or funniest moments in front of the microphone...were silence."

"Mediocre or insecure writers, directors and producers may prohibit you from taking these 'liberties' with their script, but strive for it anyway. When they hear how much life you've brought to the character, they may lose some of that paranoia about 'touching' or 'losing' some of the writer's 'precious jewels' on the page, and actually appreciate your contribution to the synergy of the production.

Also just like making music, you are part of the ensemble. [Sometimes] you are not the entire show, so it is vitally important to place yourself among all the other 'threads', which make up the 'fabric' of the production. Be professional, polite and prepared. Respect everyone else involved in a project, especially the writers. If you separate your performance form everything else in that hypothetical 'cloth,' the whole thing falls apart. When you allow everyone else to be their best, your best will shine through to its fullest potential.

Voice Acting comes from your entire body. If only your mouth is moving, that's all anyone will hear. While taking care to stay 'on mic' and not generate any other noise in the studio, freely use facial expression, hands and body in a naturally instinctive manner while you are reading your lines, no matter how silly you may think you look to the others in the room. Since the audience will never see you anyway, inhibiting your physical expression is not only unnecessary, but will invariably inhibit your vocal performance as well.

Forget about your own voice: let the *character* deliver the lines. If you are thinking about yourself, and how *you* sound, you will prohibit the character from expressing itself, making the listener aware that you are simply manipulating your voice in a hollow attempt to sound like someone else.

There is no one definitive way to deliver anything. If it's good and it works, then it is perfectly valid. (Once again, mediocre directors may only allow one specific reading they have 'formulated' in their heads to be considered 'right'; making any other choice 'wrong' in their opinion. This is, unfortunately, all too common these days.)

Avoid giving a 'cosmetic' reading: the standard, tried'n'true, expected, pedestrian interpretation which 90 percent of the world's actors normally deliver. Be thoughtful and inventive with how you use and deliver your character's [monologue or] dialogue, with respect to 'What am I actually trying to communicate?' and 'How do I really feel in this situation?'. If you are cliché in your readings, your work will be bland and undistinguished— and ultimately forgotten along with the rest of the uninspired background noise of the world."

Here's an excerpt from the same book, this time from the editors:

Daws [Butler] felt the way to make a performance interesting was through orchestration, treating the script like a piece of music.

Saying a phrase fast and then the next phrase slow, stretching out a line, mumbling a phrase, over articulating another, shouting one line and whispering the next, etc. These contrasts work but it does not matter so much where you do them as long as they feel right to you at the time. Daws would expect you to mark this book up, underline the words you want to emphasize, draw a squiggly line over a word you want to stretch out, put parenthesis [sic] around a word or phrase you want to underplay, etc. Invent your own method of orchestrating your script. Once you have done this, use it only as a guide and follow your instincts to explore the many ways to say a line as you perform it."

Here's an excerpt from Daws Butler himself:

"We do not read lines—we 'express thoughts'...in many instances, one 'thought' will wipe out another—it will take precedence, asserting its more valid importance to the continuity—this I would call 'decaying.' The end of one line seems to 'fall off' or atrophy—and the energy of the following line snaps into position. Its vitality is a refreshment—a transfusion—and it excites the listener, because it seems to be so 'natural' and spontaneous. Because it is representative of what happens in 'real life.' Remember—the actor's stock-in-trade is being 'real.' All else is pretension...Observation and sensitivity—that innate ability to take on the physical and vocal characteristics of someone else and so to lose one's self—is to become an actor...Acting is impersonation—not of celebrities—but of the world we move in. It's people. Our own sensitivity and observation of life, accumulates over the years into a memory-bank—which can be drawn upon to supply the immediate prerequisites for the particular part we are to play—to give it naturalness, distinction and belief... You never stop growing and knowing."

BIO

MARC CASHMAN is one of the few people in the commercial production business on "both sides of the glass"—as an award-winning Radio and TV commercial producer, and as a working voice actor.

President and Creative Director of Cashman Commercials, Marc creates, casts and produces music and copy advertising for radio and television. Over the past thirty-five years, he's won over 150 local, regional, national and international advertising awards, including the TELLY, ADDY, IBA, SUNNY (So. California Broadcasters), INT'L RADIO FESTIVAL OF NY, SILVER MICROPHONE, BELDING, LONDON INT'L, and the prestigious CLIO, on behalf of hundreds of ad agencies and clients across the country. His client roster has included Kroger, Charles Schwab, Quizno's, Pella Windows and Pabst Blue Ribbon Beer among many, many others.

Voted one of the *"Best Voices of the Year"* by AudioFile Magazine—three times—Marc also voices Radio and TV commercials, documentaries, animated series, video games, e-Learning modules, foreign films (dubbing) and has narrated over 100 audiobooks. Marc is currently represented by Idiom Talent Agency in Los Angeles, California, plus many other regional talent agencies around the country. He brings a high level of professionalism, humor, energy and creativity to every voice acting session.

In addition to his production schedule, he's an adjunct professor of Voice Acting at the California Institute of the Arts (Cal Arts) in Los Angeles, does pro bono work for numerous charitable and public service organizations, and instructs voice-acting of all levels through his classes through *The Cashman Cache of Voice-Acting Techniques* in Los Angeles, CA. He also coaches voice actors worldwide, produces V-O demos, and contributes articles and podcasts for NowCasting.com, Voices.com, and VoiceOverXtra.com.

Marc is a guest speaker at Advertising Federations and Broadcasters Associations throughout the U.S. and other countries, and has been the Keynote Speaker and Master Class instructor at VOICE 2008, 2010 and 2012, the international voiceover conventions held in Los Angeles, reprising those roles at VOICE 2014. He's been interviewed in numerous magazines and newspapers, radio and television programs, and is listed in Who's Who in California,

He can be contacted at 661-222-9300, via email at cashcomm @earthlink.net or his website, www.cashmancommercials.com.